PRAISING
THE HELL
OUT OF YOURSELF

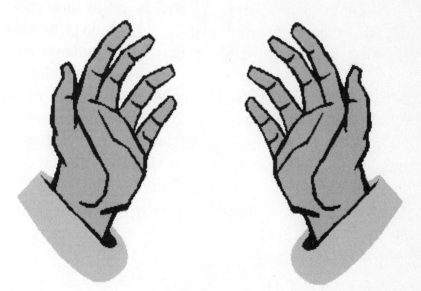

by

George O. McCalep, Jr., PhD.

PRAISING
THE HELL
OUT OF YOURSELF

Praising the Hell Out of Yourself
Copyright 2000 by Orman Press, Inc.
Lithonia, GA

ISBN: 1-891773-08-9

Printed in the United States of America

DEDICATION

I would like to dedicate this book to the following:

My wife, Sadie, who for nearly 40 years of marriage and 21 years of ministry, has stood by me in all my ventures including the writing of this book with a colorful title.

My daughter-in-law, Tracie, who has a passion for praise and the anointing to lead praise.

My children and grandchildren whom I pray that my personal praise will be a witness to them of the truth and goodness of God in Christ.

Pastor Solomon Roberts who was the first to help me come to a spiritual understanding that there is victory in praise.

To many saints of God who have discovered the joy, strength and power of praise.

And to others who have not, but I pray will be enlightened that praise should be purposeful and is beneficial.

ACKNOWLEDGMENTS

First, as always, I give all honor to the presence of the person ⟨of⟩ God who has saved me, delivered me, and inspired me to write th⟨is⟩ book.

To Rev. Christine Wells for her transcriptions.

To Minister Kay Thompson for typing the original manuscript⟨.⟩

To Sister Jackie Henderson for editing and formatting the manu⟨-⟩ script.

And to Gillespie Graphics for their creativity in designing th⟨e⟩ book cover.

TABLE OF CONTENTS

A Dramatization:
"Praising the Hell Out of Yourself"

INTRODUCTION
Praising the Hell Out of Yourself

Praising the Hell Out of Yourself is about coming into His presence with the power through praise to cast out evil. Very few Christians realize the power of praise. We have, historically, been taught the power of prayer. Although praise should always be incorporated into prayer, often it is overlooked and undervalued as an element of power. Biblically speaking, there is an interlocking relationship between strength and praise.

According to Nehemiah, "The joy of the Lord is your strength" (Nehemiah 8:10). The psalmist concurs by telling us that "Out of the mouths of babes and sucklings hast thou ordained strength because of thine enemies that thou mightest still the enemy and the avenger" (Psalm 8:2). Jesus validates and authenticates this point after implementing the courageous, strong action of cleansing the temple, turning over the table of the moneychangers, and literally chasing them out of the temple when He said, "Yea have you not read, out of the mouth of babes and sucklings thou has perfected praise?" (Matthew 21:16b). There is strength and power in praise.

Praising the Hell Out of Yourself is based on Psalm 149:6-9, which explicitly teaches us that among other purposes, praise has been given to the saints to execute vengeance and punishment on Satan and the enemies of the living God.

> *Let the high praises of God be in their mouth, and a*
> *two-edged sword in their hand; To execute vengeance*
> *upon the heathen, and punishment upon the people;*

God considers the high praises of His saints as a weapon to be used to bind up the enemy with chains and fetters of iron.

Praising the Hell Out of Yourself **is based on the theological truth that Jesus died for the penalty of sin, but the presence of sin is still with us.**

To bind their kings with chains, and nobles with fetters of iron; To execute upon them the judgment written: this honor have all his saints. Praise ye the LORD.

Notice, God considers the high praises of His saints as a weapon to be used to bind up the enemy with chains and fetters of iron. The chief enemy is the one who has already been judged. It is written that the devil will go to hell and burn in a fiery lake. There is no possible redemption for him (John 16:11). Satan's only purpose is to cause misery and find company. He is destined for hell and he would like to take others with him. This book is also based on the premise that we are not yet perfect, as we will be when He shall appear (I John 3:2). Moreover, we were born in sin and shaped in iniquity (Psalm 51:5).

The book is not intended to deny or challenge the gift of the joy of salvation. *Praising the Hell Out of Yourself* is based on the theological truth that Jesus died for the penalty of sin, but the presence of sin is still with us. We are imperfect, and in a daily battle with our fleshly sinful nature. We are now made perfect through our faith in Him; but not yet perfect in our nature.

More specifically, we are saved from Hell, but there is still a lot of Hell in us.

We will battle hell on a daily basis until we see Him face to face and become like Him. He has given us a weapon called praise, so we can keep the devil at bay and praise the Hell out of ourselves. *Praising the Hell Out of Yourself* is a book written to help in the battles of spiritual warfare. The book acknowledges the very presence of Satan in our lives. Satan is real and he is the prince of the world. We wrestle not with flesh and blood, but against principalities, against powers, against the rulers of the darkness of this world, against spiritual wickedness in high places (Ephesians 6:12).

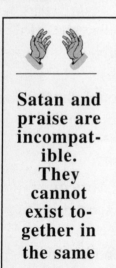

Satan and praise are incompatible. They cannot exist together in the same space.

Satan and praise are incompatible. They cannot exist together in the same space. Much like oil and water, prayer and worry are incompatible; so it is with praise and evil. When praise comes in, evil goes out. When praise shows up, evil gets out. One explanation that has some biblical basis is that before the devil got kicked out of heaven (Rev. 12:9), he had been assigned the high-ranking job of watching over the praising cherubim around the throne of God. Due to his rebellion, he was kicked out and lost his position. Therefore, whenever he hears praise, it reminds him of the cherished status that he once possessed, and it makes his flesh crawl.

You might want to test this theory by inviting someone to ride with you who does not demonstrate evidence of the fruit of the Spirit. Drive them out on the interstate at the maximum speed limit and begin to play a good praise tape or CD. Their reaction, or rather the reaction of the evil in them, should validate this viewpoint. Or from a more practical standpoint, introduce your church to praise music. Become a praising congregation. Praise can chase the hell out of church. When praise enters the church, all the evil spirits will be uncomfortable and will eventually exit.

Just as Superman is vulnerable to kryptonite, Satan is defenseless against praise.

Likewise, the evil stronghold that keeps each of us in bondage and prevents us from living the abundant, victorious life that Christ has given us, can be conquered and overcome by practicing praise as a disciple. In other words, discipline yourself to deliberately and consciously praise God according to scripture.

Just as Superman is vulnerable to kryptonite, Satan is defenseless against praise. Praise is the Achilles heel of Satan. Praise acts like a good right fist to Satan's solar plexus. Praise is a special honor, privilege and weapon God gives to the saints. However, either because of lack of knowledge, timidity or pride, saints refuse to utilize this weapon. *Praising the Hell Out of Yourself* is about how to use praise to defeat the enemy. Moreover, a deeper level of praise will result in more sin revealed in your life. Proverbs 17:3 says, *"The fining pot is for silver, and the furnace for gold: but the LORD trieth the hearts."*

Do you know what that means? It means that when you

fire up precious metal, silver or gold, the hotter these metals get, the more impurities will come to the top. Those who know how to craft know how to take impurities off the top where you can have 14K gold. The more impurities you can take off the top, the better quality of gold you will have.

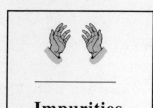

Impurities hold us back from expressing our all in praise and worship, but impurities can be burned up and out through praise.

The Bible says when we heat up in praise and worship, impurities come. In other words, we can praise the impurities out of ourselves. Even though we have cast all of our sins under the blood of Jesus, there may be something else that needs to be purged and purified by the Refiner's fire. Impurities hold us back from expressing our all in praise and worship, but impurities can be burned up and out through praise. We can literally praise the hell out of ourselves.

The story is told of a preacher who had repeatedly corrected two young boys from the pulpit who were talking and disturbing his Sunday morning sermon. After a few more verbal warnings, the preacher left the pulpit, went to the back of the church and grabbed both boys by the collar--shaking them and bumping them against each other.

When the congregation complained about the nature of the preacher's behavior, he responded by telling them if he could not preach the hell out of them, he would try to beat the hell out of them. The point is there is more than one way to battle and overcome evil in spiritual warfare. There is more than one weapon. The main offensive weapon is the sword, which is the word of God (Ephesians 6:17b). However, God has given and ordained another powerful strong weapon that is referred to as a sword called praise (Psalm 144:6b).

Biblical Examples

In the book of Joshua, praise was used to break the stronghold of Jericho. As soon as the people of God had crossed over Jordan's river, they were confronted with the stronghold of Jericho. We often sing about crossing the chilly Jordan. Spiritually we are referring to crossing from earth to heaven, or from the world to the kingdom of God. Such is indeed the case at the point of conversion. Believers have crossed over into the family of God. However, it is not unusual to receive salvation, cross over and find the devil waiting for us on the other side.

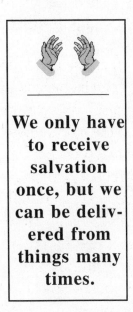

We only have to receive salvation once, but we can be delivered from things many times.

We only have to receive salvation once, but we can be delivered from things many times. Believers have strongholds that require deliverance. Jericho represents a fortress. It was tightly shut up.

Now Jericho was straightly shut up because of the children of Israel: none went out, and none came in (Joshua 6:1). God instructed Joshua and the people of God to use the power of praise to obtain the victory. God delivered the Canaanite tribe into the hands of the Israelites by the power of praise. They were instructed to participate in a faith praise march. God gave them the victory because they were obedient to His instruction to praise.

Likewise when Jehoshaphat went up against the enemy, God instructed him to go forth in praise and claim the victory.

> *And when he had consulted with the people, he appointed singers unto the Lord, and that should praise the beauty of holiness, as they went out before the army, and to say, Praise the Lord; for his mercy endureth for ever. And when they began to sing and to praise, the Lord set ambushments against the children of Ammon, Moab, and mount Seir, which were come against Judah; and they were smitten.*
> *(II Chronicles 20:21-22)*

Jonah found himself in the dangerous position of being in the belly of a whale for three days and three nights. When he offered up a sacrifice of praise/ prayer or thanksgiving, he was delivered out of his treacherous circumstance.

> *But I will sacrifice unto thee with the voice of thanksgiving; I will pay that that I have vowed. Salvation is of the Lord. And the Lord spake unto the fish, and it vomited out Jonah upon the dry land. (Jonah 2:9-10)*

Paul and Silas received deliverance from prison when they sang praises to God.

> *And at midnight Paul and Silas prayed, and sang praises unto God: and the prisoners heard them. And suddenly there was a great earthquake, so that the foundations of the prison were shaken: and immediately all the doors were opened.*
> *(Acts 16:25-26)*

Failing to use praise as a weapon against the Devil is like a soldier in a world war with a knife in his hand, allowing the enemy to choke him to death.

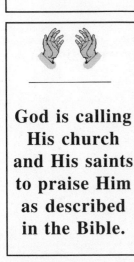

God is calling His church and His saints to praise Him as described in the Bible.

Praise is like a 3K Uuzzi Machine Gun in our hands. We have been given the privilege of firing an unlimited amount of rounds at the enemy. Failing to use praise as a weapon against the Devil is like a soldier in a world war with a knife in his hand, allowing the enemy to choke him to death. Or, it is like having a hand grenade in your hand and failing to throw it when the enemy attacks.

Or, it is like a woman being attacked by a serial rapist and failing to squirt the mace she has in her purse. Or, it is like having been trained in kung-fu and judo and allowing a bully to beat you up while you passively drop in pain. What a privilege it is to know that we can overcome evil by giving adoration to God.

God is calling His church and His saints to praise Him as described in the Bible and according to our honest and best interpretation of the scripture. *Praising the Hell Out of Yourself* is designed to instruct and inform us on how we can use praise to overcome and conquer. To accomplish this, *Praising the Hell Out of Yourself* investigates and explores these messages rendered on what the Bible says about praising. The ultimate goal of pursuing the practice of praise is that believers can praise the hell out of themselves.

Skull Practice
Introduction

1. What is the springboard scripture for *Praising the Hell Out of Yourself*?

> *Psalm 149:6-9 which explicitly teaches us that among other purposes, praise has been given to the saints to execute vengeance and punishment on Satan and the enemies of God.*

2. What theological truth is *Praising the Hell Out of Yourself* based on?

> *The theological truth that Jesus died for the penalty of sin but the presence of sin is still with us.*

3. What is the relationship between Satan and praise?

> *Satan and praise are incompatible. They cannot exist together in the same space.*

4. Does praising the hell out of yourself deny or challenge the salvation of the believer.

> *Absolutely not! Praising the hell out of yourself is about the believer using praise as a weapon in spiritual warfare.*

Fill in the blanks

1. There is strength and power in _____. (praise)

2. _____ is a weapon given to the saints to be used to bind up the enemy. (Praise)

3. Satan is defenseless against _____. (praise)

4. _____ can chase the hell out of the church.
(Praise)

What will be the outcome of ignoring the teaching in this chapter?

1. You will lose too many battles on the field of spiritual warfare.

2. Deliverance will be limited throughout your spiritual walk.

3. You will run the risk of being tied up in a spirit of bondage.

4. God will not be able to use you fully.

Helpful dialogue

1. According to the author, discuss the meaning and ramifications of Proverbs 17:3, "The fining pot is for silver, and the furnace for gold: but the LORD trieth the hearts."

2. Discuss the value of realizing and being aware of the existence of spiritual warfare. Are there members of your church that deny the reality of spiritual warfare?

3. Discuss the author's statement, "We only have to receive salvation once, but we can be delivered from many things many times."

4. Talk about the relationship between prayer and praise.

5. Discuss some biblical examples of praise used as a victorious weapon.

Chapter One
Praising The Hell Out of Yourself
Through the D-A-N-C-E

And David was afraid of the LORD that day, and said,
How shall the ark of the LORD come to me?
(II Samuel 6:9)

At some point in their spiritual walk, every believer who is serious about a growing relationship with his heavenly Father will ultimately ask the same or similar question referenced above. In the above scripture, King David asked a very important and equally timely question for the church today, "How can the ark of the Lord come to me?" In David's sincere desire for the presence of the Lord, there were several ways he could have asked this question.

For example, the question could also have been stated, "How can I come to the ark of the Lord? Or, what must I do to experience the presence of Almighty God?" You will be encouraged throughout this book to ask yourself the above question. Also, "As I diligently seek His face, how much hell from my life will be erased or need to be eradicated? What are the conditions in which He will allow me into His presence?"

A word of theological clarification is needed. Surely when we enter into the family of God by grace through faith, the presence of God the Spirit is given to us; with the promise never to leave us. So, when we talk about entering into His presence, we are talking about making more of ourseleves available to Him. We are referring to experiencing Him greater, not making Him greater. We can not make God bigger. Even when we magnify His name, we are not making Him bigger, but we are seeing and experiencing Him bigger. God can not be manipulated through praise and worship or in any other manner. He is God.

Dancing as we know it today - specifically dancing with partners either with the same or different gender - has no biblical basis.

Although we are specifically talking about praising the hell out of oneself, we are simultaneously talking about entering through the holy veil, into the very presence of God. We're talking about coming into His presence with various forms of praise & worship. In this beginning chapter, we are talking about seeking the face of God *through the d-a-n-c-e*. We dare not proceed any further with our discussion of this powerful praise weapon without looking closely at what it means to dance before the Lord. Dancing before the Lord is not only foreign to many believers, it is downright scary to others! Let me attempt to set your mind at ease.

The purpose of this chapter on dance is not to advocate that your local congregation becomes a dancing church. Neither is the purpose even to encourage or admonish you to do any dancing. As a matter of fact, dancing as we know it today - specifically dancing with partners either with the same or different gender - has no biblical basis. Also, because dancing in our society and culture is so closely associated with the world and a secular activity, we Christians must carefully weigh dancing with all scripture and biblical truth.

In I Thessalonians 5:22, God tells us to *abstain from every form of evil (NKJV)*. That command is applicable to everything, including dance. Notice the scripture doesn't just say to abstain from evil. More accurately stated, it says to abstain from ***every form*** of evil. Because that is a biblical truth, we must weigh everything we say and do against it.

Additionally, we must weigh dancing against what Paul tells us in the book of Romans:

> *But if thy brother be grieved with thy meat, now walkest thou not charitably. Destroy not him with thy meat, for whom Christ died. (Romans 14:15)*

Dancing before the Lord is a holy expression of praise that, when done from a pure heart unto the Lord, will send the devil and all of his imps scampering for a hiding place.

Here, Paul says that if eating meat will offend your brother, then you should eat no meat. Meat here represents anything lawful and moral which you desire to partake of or engage in. However, if in eating meat or participating in this desirable act, it will cause someone to miss the mark - to miss Jesus - even though it is lawful, moral and pleasurable, you should abstain from it. Just like eating meat is uncomfortable for some, dancing in church is comparably uncomfortable for others. Take heart!

Again, just like meat, God clearly approves of us participating in this act of praise when it's done in a spirit of rejoicing or spiritual warfare. This liberating form of praise allows the believer to enter into the presence of God while stripping the devil of his demonic hold over the believer's mind and will.

Dancing before the Lord is a holy expression of praise that, when done from a pure heart unto the Lord, will send the devil and all of his imps scampering for a hiding place. Dance is not just for teenagers or "steppers." Dancing is for anyone desiring the presence of God while praising the hell out of his or her life!

The dance is the most liberating.

As a believer, if you are not a participant with regard to dancing before the Lord, you may still enter through the veil into the presence of God through other acts of praise and worship. For dancing before the Lord is not the only way to enter into His presence and praise the hell out of oneself. Consequently, this chapter is about dancing, yet it is not about dancing.

This chapter, along with the others in this book, is about the various forms of praise that are acceptable and admonished by God for us to come before Him in worship. For most believers, singing is more acceptable than dancing. Singing is the most user-friendly form of praise. However, the dance is the most liberating. Remember the key is that it is acceptable to dance before the Lord, it is not acceptable to dance when your motive is dancing before others. No flesh should every glory in His presence.

Now that we know dancing before the Lord is an acceptable form of praise, let's seek to gain a better understanding of what it means to enter through the holy veil into the presence of Almighty God.

In order to do this, we must seek to understand three things: what is the holy veil; what is the ark of the covenant and its significance; and why is dance and other forms of praise pleasing to, **and desired** by God. To answer these questions, some background information is in order.

Background Information

After God delivered the children of Israel from Egyptian bondage through the leadership of Moses, He led them to Mt. Sinai. As the people of God headed toward Canaan, the Promised Land, they numbered themselves off; and according to specific instructions given to Moses by God, made for themselves what is called the Ark of the Covenant. What was the Ark of the Covenant? The Ark of the Covenant was a chest measuring approximately 45 x 27 x 27 inches and overlaid with gold.

On both sides were two pairs of rings, through which poles were slidden to make it portable. Inside the Ark were three items: the two tables of the law given to Moses (Exodus 25:16); a pot of manna (Exodus 16:33); and Aaron's rod that budded (Numbers 17:10; Hebrews 9:4). These items represented the Word of God, the promise or provision of God and the power of God, respectively. The lid of the chest was called the "mercy seat" or "place of mercy" (Exodus 25:17). The slab of gold fitted over the top of the ark had an importance all of its own.

For once every year, the high priest would enter the Holy of Holies and sprinkle the blood of bulls and goats (Leviticus 16:2-16) on the mercy seat to atone for the sins of the people. This "mercy seat" was considered a throne as it was positioned between two cherubim (winged creatures) located on opposite sides (Psalm 99:1).

The Ark of the Covenant was housed in a tent or sanctuary known as the Tabernacle. This portable tent was divided into three distinct sections: the inner court; the outer court; and the Holy of Holies. Behind the veil, in the Holy of Holies, was the residence of the Most High. Behind the veil, seated upon the mercy seat of the Ark of the Covenant, the God of Abraham, Isaac, and Jacob lived and communicated. Without question, this was God's house.

The Ark of the Covenant was so sacred, God gave Moses specific instructions on how it should be handled, and who should handle it. Because it represented the promise, provisions and power of God, the Israelites would consistently take the Ark of the Covenant to battle with them.

In doing so, they were confident that their God was **with them** during their times of war. Think about it. When they went to war, rather than running out with a flag or blowing a trumpet, they took God with them! To rid ourselves of the ravages of hell in our lives, the people of God must again desire the presence of God more than the presence of other things that are considered symbols of success or victory (i.e., money, status, degrees, big houses, etc.).

The Tabernacle and Ark of the Covenant had such an impact on the lives of the children of Israel that when Solomon built God the non-mobile temple, the same architectural design was used — an outer court, an inner court and the Holy of Holies. Even after the temple was destroyed and Haggai, Zechariah, Nehemiah, Ezra and others sought to rebuild it, the same architectural structure was used. What a powerful testimony of a people's desire to reverence the deity and holiness of God!

Behind the veil, in the Holy of Holies where the Ark of the Covenant was housed, no one except the High Priest could enter. Even he could only enter this most holy place

Because of His substitutionary sacrifice on Calvary, God no longer required the blood of goats and bulls to be sacrificed for the sins of the people behind the curtain.

after much ceremonial cleansing from his own sins. As part of his ceremonial attire, the high priest was required to wear around his waist, a type of belt with bells and fruit on it. A rope was attached to the belt.

If the high priest was unclean when he entered behind the veil and into the presence of God, he would drop dead. The priests waiting in the inner court would then drag him out from behind the veil by the rope, with the understanding that he (the high priest) entered behind the veil unprepared to meet God. Literally, no evidence of hell (the ultimate end of sin) could stand in the presence of God!

As we study the gospels, the bible teaches us that when Jesus died on the cross, not only did the sun refuse to shine, but also, rocks split open and a miniature resurrection took place. It also said that the veil in the temple, which separated the Holy of Holies from the inner court, was torn from top to bottom.

Because of His substitutionary sacrifice on Calvary, God no longer required the blood of goats and bulls to be sacrificed for the sins of the people behind the curtain. It was now possible for every man, woman, boy and girl to go into the presence of God for himself or herself. The veil was torn. The barrier was no longer there. A generational high priest was no longer needed.

The Great High Priest and Intercessor (Jesus) invites,

Every believer has the ability to enter through the veil, up to the mercy seat and into the very presence of Almighty God!

yes even encourages, us to come behind the curtain and meet God for ourselves! We can go to God for ourselves in and through our great intercessor, Jesus Christ. Every believer has the ability to enter through the veil, up to the mercy seat and into the very presence of Almighty God!

However, the question asked earlier still remains: "How can you and I, today, enter through the veil into the very presence of the living God?" One way is by dancing before the Lord.

A Biblical Example (2 Samuel 6:9)

The devil has stolen the joy of Jesus and access behind the veil out of some of our hearts.

The scripture narrative takes place after the reign of the Judges. During this era in the life of Israel, true worship was at an all time low. The children of Israel had begun to take God for granted and the Ark of the Covenant had become little more than a superstition and a ritualistic exercise.

This was the mindset of the people as they took the Ark of the Covenant out to battle against the Philistines. Because God will not be mocked by His enemies or His people, God allowed the Philistines to defeat the children of Israel and steal the Ark of the Covenant. Think about it.

The Ark of the Covenant had been stolen. What did that mean? That meant that God was stolen. The God they understood to be with them in battle was gone. Let me put it differently. Let's just say somehow or another somebody stole your Jesus. How would you feel if Jesus was stolen out of your heart? What a sad thought!

Currently, the truth of the matter is that the devil has stolen the joy of Jesus and access behind the veil out of some of our hearts. He has set up so many strongholds of hellish thoughts and activities. We must find a way to get this hell out of us! Somehow, we must find a way to regain the joy of entering behind the veil, into the presence of God where no sin is allowed. I submit to you that praise, in all of its various forms, will allow us to *Praise the Hell Out of Ourselves*, thus regaining the joy of being in the presence of God.

As we pick up on the narrative in II Samuel 6:6, we see that David is concerned about the Ark of the Covenant and restoring worship in Israel. Even though Israel was in the "land of rest," David felt there could be no rest until the Ark was returned to Jerusalem, the city of God. For seven months, the Philistines endures the wrath of God (I Samuel 6:1) and subsequently sent the Ark of the Covenant back to the Israelites on a cart driven by two oxen. The Ark ultimately landed in the home of Abinadab and there remained for twenty years (I Samuel 7:2).

King David, affectionately known as the man after God's own heart, wanted desperately to restore worship among the people. Therefore, he purposed in his heart to bring God home and set out to bring the Ark of the Covenant to the City of David from Abinadab's house. With the help of Abinadab's two sons, Uzzah and Ahio, a new cart was fashioned to transport the ark. During this relocation of

How can the ark of the Lord come to me? How then can we ever enter into His presence?

the ark, the bible records something very unusual happening. It said that the oxen stumbled and the ark began to tilt. Uzzah, probably in all good intentions, reached out to grab the Ark of the Covenant, touched it and was struck dead. God's response to Uzzah's error troubled David and led him to ask, "How can the ark of the Lord come to me?"

Now the law is interesting and I think this is why there is no record of God blessing Abinadab's house while the ark resided there. For the twenty years that the Ark was in Abinadab's house, neither David nor Abinadab studied the law to understand how to handle it. They never read God's instructions. The instructions were available in the torah, but neither of them bothered to read it.

Upon close examination of the law, we find that the Ark of the Covenant was never to be carried by some oxen. If God wanted to put it on a cart, He could have put it on a cart. But the law said that it had to be carried by the men of God, the Levites. And it was not to be touched.

David was angry. He felt it was so unjust and unfair that Uzzah had been struck dead for actions that probably were well intended. David asked the question, "How can the ark of the Lord come to me?" That's the question. How can the ark of the Lord come to me? How then can we ever enter into His presence?

How can praise and worship be restored in the hearts of the people? Until David could find an answer to his own questions, he left the Ark in the house of Obed-Edom the

Gittite (vs. 6). For three months, the ark resided in Obed-Edom's house and the Lord blessed him and all that belonged to him.

On his second attempt to bring God home, David was much more cautious. I imagine he spent time pondering many questions. Will we ever be able to come into His presence? Will we ever be able to go behind the veil into the Holy of Holies? Will we ever be able to go before the mercy seat? After obviously studying the law, David thought he would try it again—this time according to God's directions.

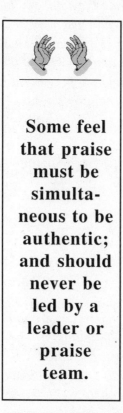

Some feel that praise must be simultaneous to be authentic; and should never be led by a leader or praise team.

In the law, David found that the Levites were suppose to carry the ark. David then prepared his praise team and trumpeters. David called in the singers and all those who could play instruments. He said we are going to let the Levites carry the ark, just like it is said in the law, and we are going to praise God as we go forth. Praise Him with the trumpet. Praise Him with singing. Praise Him with the cymbals. Praise Him with the dance!

On cue, just praise Him with one voice. Some feel that praise must be simultaneous to be authentic; and should never be led by a leader or praise team. Yet there are many biblical illustrations of praise being deliberately orchestrated. God gave Joshua specific, deliberate instructions on how to orchestrate the praise that brought down the fortified walls of the stronghold Jericho.

God told Joshua exactly how to orchestrate the praise march. God does not disapprove of orchestrated praise.

"And the Lord said unto Joshua, See, I have given into thine hand Jericho, and the king thereof, and the mighty men of valour. And ye shall compass the city, all ye men of war, and go round about the city once. Thus shalt thou do six days. And seven priests shall bear before the ark seven trumpets of rams' horns: and the seventh day ye shall compass the city seven times, and the priests shall blow with the trumpets. And it shall come to pass, that when they make a long blast with the ram's horn, and when ye hear the sound of the trumpet, all the people shall shout with a great shout; and the wall of the city shall fall down flat, and the people shall ascend up every man straight before him."
(Joshua 6:2-5)

Notice God told Joshua exactly how to orchestrate the praise march. God does not disapprove of orchestrated praise.

Likewise, God told Jehoshaphat how to orchestrate praise as a weapon against the children of Ammon and Moab.

"And Jehoshaphat bowed his head with his face to the ground: and all Judah and the inhabitants of Jerusalem fell before the Lord, worshipping the Lord. And when he had consulted with the people, he appointed singers unto the Lord, and that should praise the beauty of holiness as they went out before the army, and to say, Praise the Lord; for his mercy endureth for ever. And then they began to sing and praise, the Lord set ambushments against the children of Ammon, Moab, and Mount Seir, which were come against Judah; and they were smitten."
(II Chronicles 20:18, 21, 22)

Some think you have to get "caught up in the spirit" to praise God. However, on cue David orchestrated praise.

"When those who were carrying the ark of the LORD had taken six steps, he sacrificed a bull and a fattened calf."
(II Samuel 6:13)

Every six steps they sacrificed oxen and fatted sheep and poured out an offering unto the Lord. It must have taken them a long time to get to the City of David. Picture this in your mind, every step of the way, every six paces, they killed the fatted calf and a bullock. It must have been a bloody trail. But then they finally reached the gate of Jerusalem, the bible said that David danced before the Lord with all his might.

In fact, David danced so hard that he danced right out of his clothes. We don't know for sure, but biblical scholars think that Psalm 24 is a poetic expression of this historical event. In the 24th Psalm, it is thought that David was expressing his extreme jubilation over God coming home. The ark had been away from Jerusalem for a little over 20 years and David was excited about the presence of God being back in the midst of His people.

I can imagine what he was thinking: Here comes God to the holy city! Here comes God to Jerusalem and nobody was struck dead. We finally figured out how the ark can come unto us. We now know how we can come into the presence of God. The trumpeters are blowing and the singers are singing. The coronet and the harps are playing. In the midst of this frenzy of excitement, David in his poetic expression, brings us the 24th Psalm by saying,

"Lift up your heads, O ye gates; and be ye lift up,
ye everlasting doors; and the King of glory shall come
in. Who is this King of glory? The LORD strong and
mighty, the LORD mighty in battle. Lift up your heads,
O ye gates; even lift them up, ye everlasting doors;
and the King of glory shall come in. Who is this King
of glory? The LORD of hosts, he is the King of glory.
Selah." (Psalm 24:7-10)

Sheer celebration broke out and David danced before the Lord with all his might. The bible then says that David blessed everybody. He blessed them with drink and food and they had a great celebration. They were happy. God had come home. Their God who had been stolen and gone for over 20 years was brought home. It was celebration time, and they celebrated.   After David finished blessing the congregation, he went home to bless his family. David was feeling good and had joy in his heart. He had blessed the church and now desired to bless his children and wife. But when he got home, the bible records that his wife, Michal, had been looking out the window at the procession. She saw her husband out there in his fine kingly clothes. David had on his priestly ephod.

If you would allow me to put this in my own words, I imagine Michal said to her husband, "You sure made a fool out of yourself today! You embarrassed and humiliated me! You were out there dancing like a heathen or one of those vulgar fellows. Moreover, you pulled off your priestly clothes like you were one of those regular or servant girls down there. You made a fool out of me and yourself. You humiliated and embarrassed me. What could be so great that it could cause you to dance out of your fine, priestly clothes!"

In my imagination, I can hear David saying, "Let me tell

you something, wife. I was dancing before the Lord, the One who appointed me King—even over your father. Let me see if I can help you understand. I was dancing before the One who, just twenty years ago, kept me when I was running from your daddy, the king. Now I am king.

Let me tell you something else Michal. I was dancing before the same Lord that delivered me when I was tending my sheep and held up the bear's paw; the Lord that kept me when a lion came upon me and held his jaw shut; and the same Lord that guided the little stone that hit big Goliath and killed him. I was dancing before the Lord who has brought me a mighty long way.

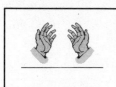

The reason dancing before the Lord is the most liberating is because it's also the most humiliating.

In fact, when I think of the goodness of the Lord and all that He's done for me, I can most assuredly say, **you ain't seen nothing yet!** I'm gonna dance some more. I'm gonna humiliate even myself. By the time I get through, I'm gonna look like a fool in my own eyes! I'm gonna *praise the hell right out of myself!*"

The context of the text here suggests that we have a problem praising God in the dance because we may humiliate or embarrass ourselves or others close to us. We have a problem humbling ourselves. The reason dancing before the Lord is the most liberating is because it's also the most humiliating.

David's wife, Michal, was embarrassed and humiliated by her husband's actions. Let's be honest, for those of us who pride ourselves in our sophistication, dancing before the Lord is quite humiliating. Thank God that God does

Dancing is one way of simply shaking off the pride that prohibits us from coming into God's presence.

not require you to dance before Him. But He does require humility. Dancing is one way of simply shaking off the pride that prohibits us from coming into God's presence. Notice Michal was not punished for not dancing before the Lord, she was punished because of her attitude about praising God with the dance.

And as the ark of the Lord came into the city of David, Michal, Saul's daughter looked through a window, and saw king David leaping and dancing before the Lord; and she despised him in her heart. Therefore Michal the daughter of Saul had no child unto the day of her death. (II Samuel 6:16, 23)

Michal had the wrong attitude about praise. However, her wrong attitude was rooted in her pride. Many church-going believers today have the wrong attitude about praise that is rooted either in pride and/or ignorance. Prayerfully, this book will help stamp out some ignorance. The deliverance from pride will have to come through the individual believer.

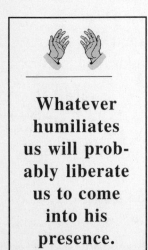

Whatever humiliates us will probably liberate us to come into his presence.

However, the good news is that God has given us a weapon of deliverance called praise. We need to be delivered from the sin of pride. We can literally praise the pride out of ourselves. Whatever humiliates us will probably liberate us to come into His presence. If we can get delivered from whatever humiliates us, it is likely that we will be freed to enter into His awesome, holy presence.

What is most humiliating to you? Crying has always been most humiliating to me. When we moved into our new church facility I got totally delivered from my humiliation of crying. It was ten years ago and God blessed us with a new, larger and beautiful church to do ministry to His glory. I had some great concerns to begin with because there was a gate that stayed locked and there was no way to pass through it. I would look at that gate and say, "When we get that church, we're gonna knock that lock off. We're going to make this church accessible to everyone."

As I was riding in an airplane, I was trying to determine what type of celebration we would have. We had planned to march from the old church to the current facility. I began receiving several suggestions on other types of things we could do. Someone suggested that we have a ground breaking ceremony.

Although a good idea, that sounded a little secular to me. Another person suggested that we have a ribbon cutting, but that sounded like celebrating the building of a federal building or a hotel. While in there in the airplane, God told me to have a veil tearing ceremony–a curtain tearing ceremony.

One Sunday School class made an Ark of the Covenant out of wood that we had to carry through the veil. Several men took a big purple curtain and draped it over a canopy. We added an orchestra, and all we needed to re-enact the Ark of the Covenant coming home. We sang and we celebrated. And then it was time to go into the facility. We had this big curtain and we thought we would do a smart thing. We rigged it with a string.

On cue, I was suppose to say a little message and somebody was to pull the string causing the curtain to tear. We were going to come into the Holy of Holies through the veil. We thought we had it all figured out. But God had another plan. Before I could give the cue, God sent a wind and the curtain tore. The wind brought it open and blew it apart and we went in and I began to cry. I remember I couldn't stop crying. I cried profusely. I shook hands and cried. I couldn't stop.

At one point in my life — like dance is to some — crying was humiliating to me. Where I come from, boys weren't suppose to cry. I can still hear my daddy's voice. My daddy used to whip me with his left hand. He called me Bud. He used to say, "Shut up Bud before I give you something to cry about." I couldn't cry.

My daddy would whip me with that left hand until I shut up in silence and then he would stop. Now I'm not suggesting that you do that. I love my daddy, but in today's time, he would get locked up for child abuse. Unfortunately, I'm afraid I would too. But the fact remains, I couldn't cry.

After my mother died when I was four years old, even though I don't remember her, I still remember the pain. I became a tough guy. All through school, I would not cry. I went to movies that were supposed to be "tear jerkers" and I just sat up there and buckled my eyes, telling myself, "I ain't gonna cry." I'm so glad God delivered me from that. Crying to me was more humiliating than dancing may be to you.

Remember, we are talking about dancing, but we aren't really talking about dancing. I humiliated myself crying.

Just as dancing is not the primary issue, neither is crying. Humility is the primary issue. The hell that pride brings had to be removed from me. When God delivers and cleanses you, seeking the face of God through praise is a natural outgrowth.

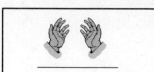

Anything that is done and you know in your heart that the motive is to draw attention to yourself, whether it's a simple waving or raising of the hand or a dance, if the purpose is to draw attention to you, it is unacceptable in the eyes of God.

Several things that we need to know about praise and worship.

1. There is an acceptable way and an unacceptable way to praise. There was an acceptable way in the Old Testament times, and there was an unacceptable way. Such is true today. But one might ask the question, what is acceptable and what is unacceptable? Without question, unequivocally, anything that involves self-grandizement is unacceptable. Anything that is done and you know in your heart that the motive is to draw attention to yourself, whether it's a simple waving or raising of the hand or a dance, if the purpose is to draw attention to you, it is unacceptable in the eyes of God.

2. Praise and Worship are marvelously interrelated, and yet different. We use these terms inter-changeably. Praise

Praise can be a one-way communication; but worship is always a two-way street.

is what we can give God; but, we can't give God worship. Praise can be a one-way communication; but worship is always a two-way street. We can praise God by ourselves, but when we worship, when we enter through the holy veil, God begins to commune with us. Praise can take place on the outside of the veil. We can praise Him in the outer court. We can praise Him in the inner court. But when we enter through the veil, somehow the liberating act of praise is translated into worship.

Praise more often precedes worship. I don't know when praise ends and worship begins. We may be praising God for a little while and somehow the interrelating work of praises to God turns into the worship of God and we find ourselves through the veil and standing before the presence of the Living God saying, "Hallelujah, thank you Lord!"

I believe that David praised Him with the trumpets, singing, pouring out of the offering, just to acknowledge who God was. Just to say, "God you are holy, sovereign and Creator. I'm just gonna praise you. But somehow or another when God came home, when God entered through the gate and David began singing "lift up your head oh you gates, be lifted up you everlasting doors," somehow or another, something got into David and he began to dance before the Lord, and He worshiped.

3. <u>Biblically speaking, the dance usually takes place when there's been deliverance.</u> We can get delivered from a

whole lot of stuff . When we say deliverance, most of us think that we are talking about just drugs and alcohol. As alluded to earlier, we can get delivered from pride. We can get delivered from self-righteousness or just looking and acting cute. We can get delivered from lust. We get delivered from over-eating, anger cursing, etc. Deliverance is something that happens to you, that you know you could not overcome yourself. The dance can be practiced for the deliverance and is a natural response to deliverance.

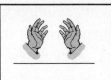

The dance can be practiced for the deliverance and is a natural response to deliverance.

We are incomplete if we do not worship God. A church is incomplete if there is no praise and worship of God.

4. <u>Christian discipleship is incomplete without worship</u>. The nation of Israel had been growing in strength since David was king. Strength was not the problem. He not only was king of the south; he was getting ready to be king of the north too. David was to be king of both kingdoms. But he knew the nation was incomplete because they did not have worship. He wanted to restore true living worship of Yahweh, the high and living God back into the nation. That's why he took some risks and tried to bring the ark back.

Likewise, we are incomplete if we do not worship God. A church is incomplete if there is no praise and worship of God. I don't care what it has achieved. I don't care how big your budget may be or how many attend Sunday School. If you don't worship, you are incomplete. It's not enough even, just to love one another. You've got to love God correctly and directly. Sooner or later you've got to enter through the veil. You can work, serve, teach Sunday School, work on committees and ministries, serve on the board, but you are incomplete if you do not worship. You cannot be a follower of God without being a worshiper.

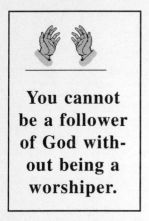

You cannot be a follower of God without being a worshiper.

You cannot be a disciple without being a worshiper. I find it interesting that over the past twenty years, there have been many in my congregation who would agree to teach Sunday School but don't want to worship. As Pastor, I had to make some decisions. I decided that if a person would not come to worship, they could not teach. Why? **Because they were incomplete!** They needed to praise the hell out of themselves.

5. <u>You must lower yourself if you are to enter through the holy veil.</u> Again, this chapter is not really about dancing. It is about lowering oneself. David said, I will humiliate myself even in my own eyes. Again, what's humiliating to you? I confessed that at one time in my life crying was humiliating to me. That may not be the case with you. The Lord set me free. I'm so free, on Christmas Eve I look for Charles Dickens' Christmas Carol to see Tiny Tim just to get me a good cry! I love to cry. God has set me free. He delivered me.

I can cry when I get ready. When something good or

bad happens, I can cry. I don't care if it's the dance or what, you must humble yourself to enter through the holy veil. It may be the dance for you. You may think that you will humiliate yourself if you get up and start dancing and twirling and putting the heel to a toe. But if that is humiliation, you might want to try it because it might get you to the mercy seat. Dancing might get you to the throne of grace, through the veil. If you want to get through the veil and praise some of the hell out of your life, you will have to humble yourself before the mighty hand of God!

Before David danced before the Lord, he sacrificed oxen and fatlings.

> *And it was so, that when they that bare the ark of the Lord*
> *had gone six paces, he sacrificed oxen and fatlings. And*
> *David danced before the Lord with all his might.*
> *(II Samuel 6:13, 14a)*

However, when I think about Jesus, and how He became our sacrifice, and how he shed His blood for me; something happens on the inside that makes my feet move on the outside. I'm glad today to be one of His dancing believers. I thank God for the power of praise through the expression of dance.

Skull Practice
Chapter One — Praising the Hell Out of Yourself Through the Dance

1. What are two important questions raised in this chapter?

(1) What must I do to experience the presence of almighty God?

(2) How much from my life will be erased or needs to be eradicated?

2. Is the dance the only form of praise that will enter me into the presence of almighty God?

No! Dancing is only one form of praise that ushers us into worship.

3. Is it necessary to be uncontrollably caught up in the spirit to dance before the Lord?

No! You can dance before the Lord at will in obedience, love and thanksgiving.

4. What are the benefits of dancing before the Lord?

Dancing before the Lord is liberating.

Fill in the blanks

1. This chapter is about seeking the face of God through the _____. (dance)

2. The purpose of this chapter is not to advocate that local congregations become _____ churches. (dancing)

3. _____ with partners, either of the same or different gender, has no biblical basis. (Dancing)

4. _____ before the Lord is a holy expression of praise that when done from a pure heart unto the Lord, will send the devil and all his imps scampering for a hiding place. (Dancing)

5. _____ is one way of simply shaking off pride that prohibits us from coming into His presence. (Dancing)

What will be the outcome of ignoring the teaching in this chapter?

1. You will limit your opportunities to enter into His presence.

2. You will miss the joy of being truly liberated.

3. You will run the risk of falling victim to one of the Bible's most deadly sins -- pride.

4. You risk the wrath of God as Michal, David's wife, experienced.

5. You will miss a joyful experience.

6. You will miss an opportunity to literally shake the devil off.

Helpful Dialogue

1. Discuss the author's statement, "Singing is the most user-friendly form of praise, however, dance is the most liberating."

2. Examine the wrong motive that results in unacceptable praise.

3. Discuss the theological significance of the tearing of the veil at the time of the crucifixion.

4. Discuss the biblical authenticity and role of the praise leader or praise team. Examine the biblical examples of praise leaders.

5. Discuss the author's statement, "Whatever humiliates us will probably liberate us to come into His presence.

6. Discuss David's wife, Michal's, attitude concerning praise and her subsequent punishment.

CHAPTER TWO
Praise the Hell Out of Yourself
With Lifted Hands

"Thus will I bless thee while I live: I will lift up
my hands in thy name. (Psalm 63:4)

Have you ever noticed how we use our hands? We clap

Our hands are an extension of our lives.

our hands when we are excited. We wave our hands when we want to get somebody's attention. We join hands when we want to be united. We hold hands when we are in love and come to the altar to be married. When we are scared, we may put our hands over our face. We raise our hands when we are happy. We put our hands together when we pray. We shake hands as a part of a greeting or to make a commitment. We clinch our hands when we're mad. We point our fingers when we really want to get someone's attention.

We use extensions of our hands for thumbs up, indicating everything is ok. We even use the finger on our hand to express a "not so holy," ugly gesture. We fold our hands when we are bored. We use our hands in many ways and to say many things. I would venture so far as to say that our hands are an extension of our lives. They reveal what we do, what we are thinking and how we feel.

In worship, hands can be used as an expression of praise. Therefore, like the dance, hands are yet another instrument in the arsenal of weapons to be used against evil.

The bible also talks a lot about hands. We use hands when we ordain somebody. We lay hands on them. In II Timothy 1:6, Paul told young Timothy

> "I remind you to stir up the gift of God which is in you
> through the laying on of my hands." (I Timothy 1:6)

Additionally, Paul wrote

> *"Therefore I desire that the men pray everywhere,*
> *lifting up holy hands, without wrath*
> *and doubting." (II Timothy 2:8)*

Hands are often considered the condition of the heart

> *"Cleanse your hands ye sinners and purify your heart*
> ye double-minded." (James 4:8)

> *"Who may ascend into the hills of the Lord and who*
> *may stand in the holy place. He who has clean hands*
> *and a pure heart." (Psalm 24:4)*

Hands represent power.

> "It is a fearful thing to fall into the hands of the
> living God." (Hebrews 10:31)

Hands bestow healing as they did in Acts 28 during Paul's journey to Malta.

> *"And it came to pass, that the father of Publius lay sick of*
> *a fever and of a bloody flux: to whom Paul entered in,*
> *and prayed, and laid his hands on him, and*
> *healed him." (Acts 28:8)*

The Bible has a lot to say about hands, but hands have

several other meanings. For example, the lifting of hands is a universal sign of surrender. If you were in a not so desirable section of a city and someone came up to you and put their finger in your back, you would probably lift your hands in an act of surrender. It is interesting that so many people, even Christians, have a problem raising their hands in God's house yet have no problem surrendering to the elements of this world! Do you realize that God is saying the exact same thing. He is saying to the church, "Stick them up!" He desires to hear Christians say, "I surrender all."

Christians have a problem raising their hands in God's house yet have no problem surrendering to the elements of this world!

The raising of hands also represents a posture of receiving, particularly when the palms are open. In sign language, the sign for "I want" is uplifted open palms. In Hebrew, the word todah, means send down a blessing and is indicated by the lifting of cupped hands. However, the praise word translation yadah, means thank you for a blessing already received and is indicated by the open-handed palm. It is possible to come to church with a todah, but if you get delivered, you could leave with a yadah. In other words, instead of seeking God for a blessing, you could thank Him for the blessings He has already given!

The same principles that apply to praising God through the dance, also apply to the use of hands in praise and worship. We should not use our hands to bring attention

We must be careful in our acknowledgment of a God-given gift that we do not begin to praise the creature more than the Creator.

To protest the lifting of hands, or any other acceptable form of praise, reflects immaturity and/or carnality.

to ourselves. We should not use the hands to steal any of God's glory. This can be easily explained as we look at how we acknowledge good performers. Because clapping in our culture is closely associated with awarding a good performance, we must recognize when we are applauding because of the message rather than the messenger.

There's nothing like an anointed saint being used by God. Whether they are singing, preaching, praying or performing drama, the message must always be pre-eminent to the messenger. God will not share His glory with anyone. Therefore, we must be careful in our acknowledgment of a God-given gift that we do not begin to praise the creature more than the Creator, or praise the gift/talent rather than He who gave the gift/talent. There's nothing wrong with acknowledging a person being used by God as long as you and the person being acknowledged recognize that "they are who they are" by the grace of God, **alone.**

While lifting holy hands may not be for everybody, no one should be condemned, prohibited, judged or criticized for entering into His presence by lifting up holy hands. This may be their way of *praising the hell out of themselves.* Far too many Christians miss the opportunity to praise God because they are too busy watching and complaining about what everybody else is doing. In fact, to protest the lifting of hands, or any other acceptable form of praise, reflects immaturity and/or carnality. Consequently, Christians should be encouraged to focus their attention on the object of their praise (Jesus). Don't worry about being the only person with raised hands. Go ahead. *Praise the Hell Out of Yourself* with your hands.

Sometimes in church, the use of our hands convey the wrong message. I once witnessed ushers opening the doors of the church with one hand resting on their hip. As I continued to watch, I wondered what message was being conveyed to those entering to worship. "Don't come in. Don't get close to me. We really don't want you here. I don't want to be here and I can't imagine why you do!" Because our hands are an extension of who we are and what we are thinking and feeling, we must always recognize that our hands can be used to usher someone into the presence of God or repel them from Him.

Interestingly enough, it appears that we can use our hands to do everything else **except praise God.** We do a wave in our sports stadiums when we get excited about our favorite team or player. Some believers feel that we don't want to bring the superdome mentality into the church. The truth is that the sports world stole the wave from the Church. Read the books of Exodus and Leviticus. God told the people to bring Him a **wave offering.** Literally, take your offering, lift your hand and wave it to Me. Therefore, more than 10,000 years ago, people were lifting their hands doing the wave!

Like many other things, the world has stolen from the church and we refuse to take it back to the glory of God. If we can raise our hands for someone who runs up and down a field or court - someone who doesn't even know our names, how much more lifting of hands does the One who knows how many hairs are upon our heads deserve!

Some will not lift their hands because they do not want to be known as a fanatic. Often when I go home after church, my grandson will be waiting for me. When I arrive at home and walk in the door, he will come running to me, with his hands outstretched saying, "Granddy is home! Granddy is home!" I don't say to him, "Put your hands down. Don't be a fanatic, boy!" I find it difficult to believe that any parent or grandparent would deny any child that seeks to be held and in the presence of the one they love the opportunity to be in their presence.

The lifting of hands, like the dance, may not be for everyone. However, as a Pastor and fellow Christian, I highly recommend it. Our hands are a part of our everyday life. We use them to work, play, eat, and write. Why not use them to praise God! Try it! You might like it! You might find a new expression of joy in your life that will aid you in *praising the hell out of yourself!*

One of the ways of praising God for His cleansing power is by raising our holy hands for all the world to see!

After all, who gave you your hands. It is He (God) who made us and not we ourselves. In recognition of that fact, we must also realize that God didn't just give us our hands. He made them holy. And since He made them holy, we should be the more cautious about what we do with them and where we put them. I know that I am not the only person who has ever had some dirty hands and been ashamed of where they had been. But yet, God took my dirty hands and cleaned them up in His righteousness. By faith, even my hands are made right. Now I can come into His sanctuary and raise holy, **clean** hands. One of the ways of praising God for His cleansing power is by raising our holy hands for all the world to see!

There are three spiritual truths that we must explore regarding the lifting of holy hands in praise unto God.

God's Party

Worship is God's party. I think some of us get this fact backwards. When we go to church, some of us act as though we think it is our party. We expect a little entertainment out of the choir. We come and we sit calmly, and the choir sings.

We expect to be entertained like it's our party. If the truth be told, some of us want a little entertainment out of the Pastor. If he can't entertain us, he hasn't really preached. However, worship is God's party. God is the One who is to be entertained. He is the One who we go to church to meet. He is the One that made us for His good pleasure.

"Thou art worthy, O Lord, to receive glory and honour and power: for thou hast created all things, and for thy pleasure they are and were created." (Revelation 4:11)

Praise is a gift to God at His party.

Since worship is God's party, it stands to reason that we should bring something of meaning to the party as a gift for the honoree. The only gift that He asks for and that we are capable of giving is praise. Praise is a gift to God at His party. Like other party gifts given, we should be concerned as to whether or not our gift was pleasing to God. We should examine our gift and at least ask the honoree is he was pleased with our party gift.

Because God is just a gracious loving party host, He permits us to party at his party. He even provides party favors for our needs. We are forever stuffing our pockets with party favors from God's party. On a deeper level, these party favors satisfy basic human needs. In a lecture given by my friend, Dr. Nathan Johnson, these basic needs were listed and described as follows:

> **Because God is just a gracious loving party host, He permits us to party at his party.**

1. The need for finiteness to seek infiniteness. In worship, we seek completion through communion with God. Sensing our limitations, we go in search for the rest of ourselves.

2. The need to satisfy a sense of mystery seeking understanding. We seek to come into His presence for knowledge that unlocks the mysteries of life.

3. The need to satisfy a sense of insecurity seeking refuge. In an age of uprootedness, we realize our need for refuge and stability. God provided a party favor of refuge at His party.

4. The need to satisfy a sense of loneliness that seeks compromising with God. In our estrangement and our loneliness, we feel the need to be loved. Worship is a search for this love, which can satisfy our loneliness. A choice

Party-pop-pers often destroy this sense of satis-faction be-cause of their unwillingness to bring some praise to God's party.

party favor is to experience personal companionship with God.

5. The need to satisfy a sense of human belonging that seeks mutual fellowship with other worshipers. This party favor is an outgrowth of "not forsaking the assembly of God" and partaking together at God's party. Party-poppers often destroy this sense of satisfaction because of their unwillingness to bring some praise to God's party.

6. The need to satisfy a sense of guilt that seeks forgiveness and absolution. In worship, our soul is laid bare before God. We acknowledge our guilt and plead for cleansing.

7. The need to satisfy a sense of anxiety that seeks peace. Anxiety is a normal experience of human finiteness. In this deep threat of non-being, we seek to worship Him and the courage to become our true selves. As emotional tensions build up, we seek peace from them in the deepest of all emotional experiences - worship. This emotional experience can reach to the depths of our need for rest and peace.

8. The need to satisfy a sense of meaningless that seeks purpose and fulfillment. The search for meaning is perhaps our deepest need. In the depths of our soul we realize that we were created for a purpose. The search for meaning finds its deepest significance in worship.

And we know that God causes everything to work together for the good of those who love God and are called according to his purpose for them. For God knew his people in advance,

*and he chose them to become like his Son, so that his Son would
be the firstborn, with many brothers and sisters. And having
chosen them, he called them to come to him. And he gave
them right standing with himself, and he promised them his
glory. (Romans 8:28-30)*

9.   The need to satisfy brokenness that seeks healing.
We cannot grapple with the enemies of righteousness in a
realistic world without becoming broken and bruised.

10. The need to satisfy a sense of grief that seeks comfort. Our innumerable losses leave us with a feeling of
emptiness. *"Comfort, comfort my people, says your God"
(Isaiah 40:1). (Source: Lecture given by Dr. Nathan
Johnson, entitled "Transforming Lives Through Worship"
given at the Institutional Missionary Baptist Conference
of America, March 15, 2000)*

The   above 10 basic needs that are satisfied through
worship indeed can be thought of as party favors. God
provides them for us at His party. But the favors are not
automatic. You must first come to the
party with a sacrificial gift of praise to
receive the favors. Coming before Him
with uplifted hands is one way of receiving the party favors of God in worship.

**Worshiping
God is just
as important
as working
for God.**

Worshiping God Vs Working for God

Worshiping God is just as important
as working for God. Worshiping God is just as important
as serving God. Oftentimes, we find Christians who don't

mind serving in the church, even teaching Sunday School, but have a problem worshiping. As Pastor, I have this problem. You can't be a worker unless you are a worshiper. Sometimes we even make a mistake in the way we assimilate new members. When somebody joins the church, one of the first things we do is "get them involved in the ministry."

When we worship Him, we love Him and make love to Him.

In other words, we put them to work. Maybe the first thing we need to do is teach them how to be a worshiper rather than placing so much emphasis on becoming a worker. After all, the first commandment is to love thy Lord thy God with all thy heart and with all thy mind and with all thy soul. When we worship Him, we love Him and make love to Him. He meets us in love and in communion in our spirits.

Before we start working, we should start worshipping. If you love someone, you will serve them. Oftentimes, people come into church on fire and say, "I want to work. What can I do?" They start off and they're hot. About six months later, they are no where to be found. Their fire has fizzled out, or stated another way, "they are burned out." The church has too many members with Alka Seltzer religion. The problem is that they are not fueling on the right type of fuel. Serving may bring you gratification for a while. But serving without worshipping will eventually cause you to burn out. One only has to look at the example shown us in the gospel according to Luke:

"Now it came to pass, as they went, that he entered into a certain village: and a certain woman named Martha received him into her house. And she had a sister called Mary, which also sat at Jesus feet, and heard his word. But Martha was cumbered about much serving, and came to him, and said, Lord, dost thou not care that my sister hath left me to serve alone? Bid her therefore that she help me. And Jesus answered and said unto her, Martha, Martha, thou art careful and troubled about many things. But one thing is needful: and Mary hath chosen that good part which shall not be taken away from her." (Luke 10:38-42)

Loving God is the first and greatest commandment; therefore worshiping God (giving adoration to God) ought to take priority.

Notice Jesus did not reprimand Martha for serving. If you are sure you will serve, and it pays to serve Jesus. However, loving Jesus precedes serving Jesus. Mary was found sitting at Jesus' feet, worshiping Him. Mary chose the "good part". Martha was working trying to get things right for Jesus, but Mary was found getting right with Jesus. Believers must get right, stay right with Jesus, and prepare Him. Worshiping and loving Jesus is the "good part."

Loving God is the first and greatest commandment; therefore worshiping God (giving adoration to God) ought to take priority. On another occasion, recorded in John 12:3-5 and 8, another Mary was found loving God demonstratively, and others could not understand the importance of the priority placed on worshiping God.

"Then took Mary a pound of ointment of spikenard, very costly, and anointed the feet of Jesus, and wiped his feet with her hair: and the house was filled with the odour of the ointment. Then saith one of his disciples, Judas Iscariot, Simon's son, which should betray him. Why was not this ointment sold for three hundred pence, and given to the poor. For the poor always ye have with you; but me ye have not always."

Once again, Mary chose the "good part--worship". Notice the disciple Judas Iscariot could not understand the necessity to prioritize worship. Like Judas, who later betrayed Jesus, believers today who do not prioritize expressive worship (raising hands, bowing down, etc.) are betraying God's command to praise and worship Him. Believers who suffer from this Judas syndrome could bring themselves back into a perfect relationship with Jesus by praising the hell out of themselves. If Christians would spend more time sitting at His feet, learning of and from Him, lifting holy hands would not need to be encouraged. It would be a natural expression of the love relationship with Christ. God desires us more than He desires our works!

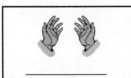

Reaching up is just as important as reaching out. Whether you are reaching up or out, the implication is that the hands are being used.

Loving God Vs Loving Each Other.

We serve a vertical and horizontal cross. Some of us want to serve a vertical cross only while others of us seek to serve a horizontal cross only. The vertical cross alone reaches up and communes with God but becomes pharisaical when the love and presence of God is not given away. The horizontal cross alone reaches out to people but lacks the power to bring about sustained, healthy growth because it is generated by human effort.

Reaching up is just as important as reaching out. Whether you are reaching up or out, the implication is that the hands are being used. God loves and desires us to reach up to Him in humble surrender, and reach out to others in compassion. Holy hands can and should be used for both.

In summary, we are reminded of the holy hands of Jesus. The hands that minister and heal on the dusty roads of Palestine. The hands that the disciples on the road to Emmaus saw that caused them to turn around and head back towards the cross. After they declared "Did not our hearts burn when He opened up the scriptures before us."

And it came to pass, as he sat at meat with them, he took bread, and blessed it, and brake and gave to them. And their eyes were opened, and they knew him; and he vanished out of their sight. And they rose up the same hour, and returned to Jerusalem, and found the eleven gathered together, and them that were with them. (Luke 24:30-33)

Jesus used His hands to disciple the Kingdom of Heaven when he laid hands on the little children and blessed them.
And they brought young children to him, that he should touch them and his disciples rebuked those that brought them.
(Mark 10:13)

Jesus used Thomas' hands on His second visit to the Upper Room (after His Resurrection) to cause Thomas to be transformed from a doubter to a believer, and cry out - "My Lord, and My God."
Then saith he to Thomas, Reach hither thy finger, and behold my hands; and reach hither thy hand, and thrust it into my side: and be not faithless, but believing. And Thomas

answered and said unto him, My Lord and my God.
(John 20:27-28)

I am further reminded of the lifted up, pierced hands of Jesus at the cross when he died for your sins and my sins and the sin of the world. With pierced, bleeding hands, He said, "Father forgive them for they know not what they do...[and] Father into thy hands I commend my spirit."

The picture of pierced hands is not the last picture of Jesus' hands. For we indeed confess that on the third day he got up from the grave with all power in His hands. When we think of the hands of Jesus, we ought lift up our hands in surrender to Him and love for Him. Lifting up Holy Hands is indeed lifting Him up, and He has declared that "if I be lifted up, I will draw all men unto Me." Uplifted hands can be tools of evangelism, and an instrument for expression of love and admiration to God; as well as a weapon against the evil forces in the world which often evade us.

Skull Practice
Chapter Two — Praising the Hell Out of Yourself With Lifted Hands

1. Can the lifting of hands be an acceptable form of praise?
Yes, as long as they are used to acknowledge, adore, and glorify God.

2. Can hands be used as an unacceptable form of praise?
Yes, when our hands are used to bring attention to ourselves.

3. Do the holy scriptures speak to the use of hands as an instrument of praise?
Yes! Study the following scriptures: 1 Timothy 28; 2 Timothy 2:8; James 4:8; Psalm 63:4.

4. What are some of the ways hands are used in the Bible?
(1) to praise (Psalm 63:4)
(2) to ordain (1 Timothy 1:6)
(3) to describe a condition of the heart (James 4:8
      and Psalm 24:4)
(4) to heal (Acts 28:8)

Fill in the blanks

1. _____ are an extension of our lives. (Hands)

2. _____ are an indicator of the condition of the heart. (Hands)

3. Lifting of _____ is a universal sign of surrender. (hands)

4. The raising of _____ also represent a posture of receiving, particularly when the palms are open. (hands)

5. In worship _____ can be used as an expression of praise. (hands)

What will be the outcome of ignoring the teaching in this chapter?

1. You will continue to use your hands for survival, yet never surrender them to God.

2. You will not fully enjoy the party or the party favors at God's party.

3. You run the risk of not bringing God a pleasing gift to His party.

4. You run the risk of being a party pooper at God's party.

Helpful dialogue

1. Discuss how the world of sports stole the wave from the church.

2. Discuss the implication of worship being God's party rather than our party.

3. From a needs perspective, discuss the author's statement, "We are forever stuffing our pockets with party favors from God's party."

4. Discuss worship in relationship to the first and greatest Commandment.

Chapter Three
Praising the Hell Out of Yourself With Thanksgiving

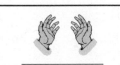

Praising God should not be difficult or something a "Praise Team" should have to beg Christians to do.

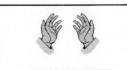

If you can think, you can thank; if you can thank, you can praise; if you can praise, you can worship.

Enter into his gates with thanksgiving; and into his courts with praise: be thankful unto him, and bless his name.
(Psalm 100:4)

Think, thank, praise and worship. In Psalm 100:4, God tells us these very simple words of instruction, admonition and command. He says, "Enter into My gates with thanksgiving and into My courts with praise: be thankful unto Me and bless My name." Praising God should not be difficult or something a "Praise Team" should have to beg Christians to do.

Additionally, the instructions of Almighty God are not complex. All one has to do is to reflect on the character and goodness of God. If those thoughts alone do not draw you into an "attitude of gratitude," a remembrance of all the dirt and filth God stepped into and lifted you out of should cause a "crazy praise" to swell up in you.

If you can think, you can thank; if you can thank, you can praise; if you can praise, you can worship. If you can't praise, then there is something wrong with your thinking.

One songwriter puts it this way, "When I look back over my life and I think things over, I can truly say that I've been blessed. I've got a testimony." As Christians, we must often look back over our lives and think things over as we interpret what we see through the eyes of faith and thanksgiving.

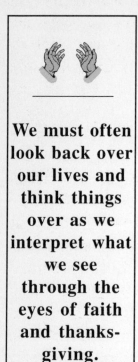

We must often look back over our lives and think things over as we interpret what we see through the eyes of faith and thanks-giving.

When we interpret just how the Lord has brought us and all the marvelous things He has done, we will thank Him! If you thank Him long enough, you'll desire to praise Him! If you praise Him long enough, you will find yourself behind the curtain, in the Holy of Holies standing before the mercy seat worshiping God in the beauty of holiness.

That is really what the Psalmist is saying in the 95th through the 100th Psalms. The Psalmist is simply looking back over his life. David, the psalmist, is looking back and thinking things over. He is reflecting on just how far the Lord brought him and how good God has been to him. David concludes his reflection with,

> *"The Lord is good; His mercy is*
> *everlasting;*
> *and His truth endureth to all*
> *generations."*
> *(Psalm 100:5)*

I often wonder what David was thinking about during the time he penned these particular psalms. Maybe he was thinking of the time when he was a little shepherd boy tending his father's flock and a bear came upon him and the flock, and again, God's mercy and power gave him the victory! Or maybe he was reflecting over the time God used a pebble and a sling to bring down Goliath. Not even the most sophisticated guidance missile system man could develop could strike with such accuracy. Only the hand of **God** can aim that straight!

Maybe David wasn't thinking about those situations. Maybe he was thinking about the time when King Saul hunted him like a fugitive, like a master would search for a runaway slave. Or maybe he was thinking about committing adultery with Bathsheba and murder against her husband, Uriah. Death, according to David, should have been punishment.

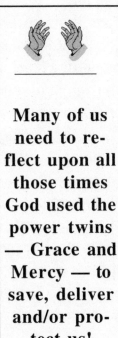

Many of us need to reflect upon all those times God used the power twins — Grace and Mercy — to save, deliver and/or protect us!

Yet, God spared his life. I'm not really sure what David was really thinking about. What I do know, however, is that many of us need to reflect upon all those times God used the power twins — Grace and Mercy — to save, deliver and/or protect us! The shear thought of any of those situations should cause one to begin *praising the hell out of themselves.*

I can remember growing up as a little boy in Alabama. On one occasion, I slid off the hay wagon and at what appeared to be the last moment before I would be seriously injured or killed, one of the men reached down and grabbed me. I recognize that it was the hand of God that allowed me to be alive today. I can think back to the time I was a teenager, rolling a wheel barrow out of a building. Just as I exited the building, the entire upper structure of the building collapsed. Yet, I am here today.

As I interpret those and so many similar situations through the eyes of faith, an attitude of thanksgiving wells up inside of me. Therefore, worship is a reflective experience. It is a reflective, objective experience that is the outgrowth of reflecting (thinking) about God. And worship is also a reflective, subjective experience when we reflect (think) about ourselves in reference to God.

If we are honest, all of us have been delivered by the hand of God many times. We need to start "thinking things over." For example, maybe you were fornicating against the Word of God. Maybe you were defiling your body by putting stuff in it that didn't belong there. Several years ago, a young basketball player with an extremely promising sports future put cocaine in his body. The impact of that decision was tragic! The intensity of the drug was too much for the young man's heart and he died almost instantly.

I wonder how many times other individuals have put items such as alcohol, marijuana, crack, cocaine, prescription drugs, too much food, tobacco, or any number of harmful things into their body, not realizing that their heart may have been one beat away from the last beat! Thank God for His grace and mercy. As we look back through the eyes of faith, we very well understand why David said,

Make a joyful noise unto the Lord, all ye lands. Serve the Lord with gladness: come before his presence with singing. Know ye that the Lord he is God: it is he that hath made us, and not we ourselves; we are his people, and the sheep of his pasture. ***Enter into his gates with thanksgiving, and into*** *his courts with praise: be thankful unto him, and bless his* ***name.*** *For*

the Lord is good; his mercy is everlasting; and his
truth endureth to all generations.
(bold emphasized by author)
(Psalm 100)

Notice first, David admonishes everybody (all ye lands) to make a joyful noise, unto the Lord. "All ye lands" means **everybody**. There's one problem here. Noise bothers some Christians. The word "noise" simply means "noise." We are to be noisy in our joyful thanksgiving to God.

The bible then goes on to say, *"Serve Him with gladness."* God doesn't want you to serve Him with a long face or begrudgingly. We are to serve him with gladness, not madness. We should be **glad** to serve Him. Remember, look back over your life and think things over! I have seen so many serving in the church with sour looks on their faces. Some of us even come to church looking like we just sucked a lemon! But God said to serve Him with gladness. To reflect simply on God himself should cause us to desire to serve Him with gladness. However, if we take that a step further and think about the many rewards He has poured out upon us, the only time a frown should be on our faces is when we have sucked on a lemon.

Then we are to enter into His presence with singing. Everybody can sing. Singing is the most user-friendly of all forms of praise. It (singing) alone can cause a person to *praise the hell out of him/herself.* Therefore, I have dedicated an entire chapter, which will be discussed later, on praising the hell out of yourself with singing.

After we recognize that God made us and we didn't make ourselves, we are to enter into His gates with thanksgiving, and into his courts with praise. We are to be thankful unto Him and bless His name. Why? Because the Lord is good and His mercy is everlasting and His truth endureth to all generations. What is the truth about God that will endureth throughout eternity? The truth is, He is good. His mercy is everlasting. He is sovereign. He is immutable (unchanging). He is loving. He is forgiving. He is longsuffering. He is all-powerful. He is all-knowing. He is the Creator who is blessed for evermore. He is our shield and exceedingly great reward. He is our healer. He is our Source of unlimited supply...get the point! Think about it and start thanking Him! If you can think, you can thank; if you can thank, you can praise; and if you can praise, you can worship.

If We Know Better, We Should Do Better

With all that has been said, the question begs to be asked, "If we know these things and still don't do them, what's our problem?" Why don't we give God the praise He alone is worthy to receive? I submit to you that, quite simply, we are stiff-necked, ungrateful and disobedient to the Word of God, the root of which is pride. We want just a little of it. Look what the book of Romans says about that.

"Because that, when they knew God, they glorified Him not as God,
neither were thankful; but became vain in their imaginations,
and their foolish heart was darkened. Professing themselves to be
wise,they became fools, and changed the glory of the incorruptible
God into an image made like to corruptible man, and to birds, and
fourfooted beasts, and creeping things. Wherefore God also gave
them up to their uncleanness through the lusts of their own hearts,
to dishonor their own bodies between themselves: Who changed
the truth of God into a lie, and worshiped and served the creature
more than the Creator, who is blessed for ever. Amen."
(Romans 1:21-25)

We have become vain in our imaginations and want somehow to believe that we are wise enough to take care of ourselves, thereby making us worthy of a little glory.

Herein lies our problem. We have made God out of a lie. We have become vain in our imaginations and want somehow to believe that we are wise enough to take care of ourselves, thereby making us worthy of a little glory. Ridiculous! I don't care how much talent a person has. His name could be Michael Jordan, Barry Sanders, Mother Teresa, Donald Trump or President So-and-So, God is the Maker and Creator who is blessed forevermore! He made that person the way he or she is.

Whether you're the greatest scholar that will ever live or the most skilled surgeon who ever performed an operation, God is still the Maker, Creator and Sustainer. He is the One who allowed us to be who we are. It doesn't matter whether you were a good little girl or boy, never got in trouble at school, never fornicated, was a virgin when you got married, never smoked a cigarette (not to mention a joint), or never tasted alcohol upon your lips, if you believe you accomplished any of those achievements on your own, you are vain and calling Almighty God a liar. Watch out! You are thanking and worshiping yourself (the creature) rather than God (the Creator). No flesh should glory in his presence. This is the reflective, objective thinking mentioned earlier. This is reflection on who God is.

How then do we change our thinking? First, we recognize

that to know God is to worship God.   Again, Psalm 100:3 gives us a little clue. It says,

> *"...know ye that the Lord, He is God. It is*
> *He that hath made us and not we ourselves."*

The virgin ought to be able to make as much of a joyful noise as the prostitute!

To praise God requires a move out of natural or normal comfort zones.

That is simple and yet so profound. It is so simple that we often don't understand it. If you know that He is God and it is He that made usk then you will not try to take any credit for being a great mathematician or musician. Objective, reflective thinking will bring you into an experience that will quickly eliminate the ungodly thinking that one person is better than another because of who they know or what they have or have not done.

Therefore, the virgin ought to be able to make as much of a joyful noise as the prostitute! The prostitute may be shouting about where God has brought her from. The virgin should be shouting about the fact that only God was able to keep him/her from giving into the temptation of premarital sex!

It's all the same joyful noise in the ears of God. The joyful noise of the addict should be the same as that of the non-addict. You must recognize that the only reason you are the way you are is because **it is He (God) who made (and kept) us and not we ourselves!**

If you think about it long enough, you'll thank Him. If you thank Him long enough, you'll praise Him. If you praise Him long enough, some of the hell in your life will disappear. And if you hang in there during the time of intense praise, you'll find yourself behind the curtain, in the Holy of Holies, in the middle of the presence of Almighty God. To praise God requires a move out of natural or normal comfort zones. If the natural or normal characteristic is one of aggression or egotism, you must humble yourself to give God what He desires. If the barrier is shyness, that natural characteristic too must be removed. I have heard so many people say, "I can't raise my hand or say hallelujah out loud because I'm too shy." God requires us to move out of our excuses into obedience in order to praise Him the way He desires.

The scripture teaches us that the outward visible is required just as much as the inner spiritual worship of the soul.

Humility is required to worship God. Therefore, all pride must be removed from your heart. God worked a miracle in my life. My natural personality was and still is a loner. I like to be alone. I like to eat alone. If I had my way, I would read a book, watch a ball game, eat a ham sandwich, lemon pie and a little ice cream — completely alone!

But God knew that I could not pastor a church and be a loner. He knew that I needed to be able to greet people, shake hands, hug necks and remember names. God worked a miracle in me by delivering me out of my comfort zone. For us to praise God the way He desires as well as being used by Him,

we must step out of our comfort zones and natural per-
sonalities.

Let me tell you about another thing that I know where
believers struggle. The scripture teaches us that the outward visible is required just as much as the inner spiritual
worship of the soul. The bible says,

> *"O come let us worship and bow down: let us kneel*
> before the Lord our maker." *(Psalm 95:6)*

This suggests the demonstrative action of the body in
worship to God. Oh yeah, sometimes it helps the inner
soul but it is **required** by God that we raise holy hands and
bow down before Him. God requires that we sing aloud to
Him, as well as demonstrate other forms of praise and worship discussed in this book. It is **required** by God for us
to honor Him with our bodies in praise and worship. Luke's
gospel records a sinner woman worshiping Him with body
and soul.

> *"And, behold, a woman in the city, which was a sinner, when*
> *she knew that Jesus sat at meat in the Pharisee's house,*
> *brought an alabaster* box of ointment, And stood at his feet
> behind him weeping, and began to *wash his feet with tears,*
> *and did wipe them with the hairs of her head, and kissed*
> *his feet, and anointed them with the ointment."*

She not only bowed her body but she kissed His feet,
and washed His feet with the tears that came from her heart
and soul. Then she anointed them with ointment. In my
opinion, this sinner woman thought about the goodness of
Jesus, and was thankful just to be in His presence; therefore, she entered into a loving expression of praising the
hell out of herself.

Skull Practice
Chapter Three -- Praising the Hell Out of Yourself With
Thanksgiving

1. What is the relationship between thanksgiving and praise?

Praise is the result of an attitude of gratitude.

2. Are thanksgiving and praise suggestions or commands?

Commands! God tells us to "Enter His gates with thanksgiving and His courts with praise."

3. What is meant by the statement that "Worship is a reflective experience"?

Worship is an experience of that which is the outgrowth of thinking about God.

4. What is the root sin that keeps us from thinking, thanking, praising and worshiping God as we should?

The root of this sin is pride.

Fill in the blanks

1. If you can think, you can _____. (thank)

2. We must look back over our lives and think things over as we interpret what we see through the eyes of faith and _____. (thanksgiving)

3. After we recognize that God made us and we did not make ourselves, we are to enter His gates with _____. (thanksgiving)

4. If you can _____, you can praise. (Thank)

What will be the outcome of ignoring the teaching in this chapter?

1. You will be disobedient to His word and will.

2. You will be an ingrate in the eyes of God.

3. You run the risk of serving Him with sadness rather than with gladness.

4. You run the risk of stealing some of God's glory.

Helpful dialogue

1. Discuss the author's statement, "The virgin ought to be able to make as much of a joyful noise as the prostitute!"

2. Discuss and reflect on your personal comfort zones and how a higher level of thanksgiving may help you move out of them.

3. Discuss the author's assertion that if you can think, you can thank; if you can thank, you can praise; if you can praise, you can worship.

4. Discuss the implication of the scriptural teaching that the outward visible worship is regarded just as much as the inner spiritual worship.

Chapter Four
Praising The Hell Out of Yourself
With Righteousness
And a Holy Offering

"But ye are a chosen generation, a royal priesthood,
an holy nation, a peculiar people; that ye should
shew forth the praises of him who hath called you out
of darkness into his marvelous light" (I Peter 2:9)

Because of our identity as believers, we must understand that all of us possess the ability to enter the Holy of Holies, and into the presence of God.

The bible tells us that all believers are priests. This is known as the doctrine of the priesthood of believers. The bible also declares that we are a holy nation, a royal priesthood, a peculiar people. Because of our identity as believers, we must understand that all of us possess the ability to enter the Holy of Holies, and into the presence of God.

Our great Intercessor and Advocate, Jesus Christ, secured our access to the Father when the curtain at the back of the temple was torn when He died on the Calvary's Cross.

Remember from previous chapters, prior to this act, only the High Priest could go behind the curtain, and this was only accomplished after much ritualistic cleansing and sanctifying.

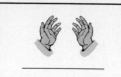

Praise cannot be effectively administered and received by God without righteousness.

Although we do not have to do any ritualistic cleansing, we also must be clean before going through the veil into the presence of God. Therefore, we must come into His presence with righteousness. Praise cannot be effectively administered and received by God without righteousness. The good news is that,

'If we confess our sins, he is faithful and just to forgive us our sins, and to cleanse us from all unrighteousness."
(I John 1:9)

Even as the Levites of the Old Testament had to be cleansed, so must we before entering God's presence. You cannot go behind the curtain dirty. You can't enter into God's presence with unrighteousness. We must never think that praise is an act of substitution for confession. We make a mockery of ourselves and disappoint our Heavenly Father, when we praise Him, knowing we have not sought righteousness. Actually, we make fools of ourselves when we attempt to approach God in praise, and yet we have not made confession concerning the sin in our lives.

In the year King Uzziah died, the Prophet Isaiah heard the voice of God. Before he heard the voice, however, he saw the Lord high and lifted up. Isaiah's first conclusion was that he was a man of unclean lips. He had to confess that he was also among a people of unclean lips.

'In the year the king Uzziah died I saw also the Lord sitting upon a throne, high and lifted up, and his train filled the temple...Then said I, Woe is me! for I am undone; because I am

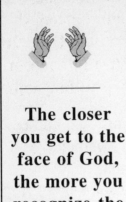

The closer you get to the face of God, the more you recognize the *hell that needs to be praised out of your life.*

a man of unclean lips: for mine eyes have seen the King, the Lord of hosts." (Isaiah 6:1, 5)

The text continues on to describe how a cherubim flew off of the holy place with a hot coal, purging him of his sins. Then and only then did he hear the voice of the Lord asking who will go for Him and who should He send. The closer you get to the face of God, the more you recognize the *hell that needs to be praised out of your life.* In fact, God desires to completely clean up His royal priesthood so that He can use them in a glorious manner.

David, the primary author of the Psalms, is again a grand example of a person who recognized the need for righteousness. In many ways, David reminds me of myself. He was the greatest sinner and saint of the Old Testament. He did his share of sinning. But he obviously did his share of confessing and repenting as well. Long before he danced before the Lord, David raised the questions,

"Lord, who shall abide in thy tabernacle? who shall dwell in
*thy holy hill? He that walketh uprightly, and worketh
righteousness, and speaketh the truth in his heart."*
(Psalm 15:1-2)

*"Who shall ascend into the hill of the Lord? or who shall
stand in his holy place? He that hath clean hands, and a
pure heart; who hath not lifted up his soul unto vanity, nor sworn
deceitfully. He shall receive the blessing from the Lord,*
and righteousness from the God of his salvation." (Psalm 24:3-5)

David obviously recognized the need for righteousness as well as the only One who could make him righteous! The bible tells us that our faith makes us right with God. However, before we can be made right, we must first repent and confess our wrong. Jesus began His early preaching ministry with a call for repentance.

"From that time Jesus began to preach, and to say, Repent: for the kingdom of heaven is at hand." (Matthew 4:17)

No transformation of cleaning takes place without first repenting. When the prophet Nathan revealed to David his sin relative to Bathsheba and Uriah, David repented.

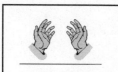

You cannot praise the hell out of yourself until you first repent of the hell in yourself.

"And David said unto Nathan, I have sinned against the Lord." (II Samuel 12:13a)

There can be no true revival without repentance. Church never breaks out deep down in the bottom of our souls without us first truly being sorry enough for our past wrongs. We must ask God to turn us around in our tracks. Evidence of repentance is turning around and heading in another direction.

I am afraid many of us come to church Sunday after Sunday and hear a transforming word from God, but no transformation takes place in our lives. Why? Because we refuse to repent. You cannot praise the hell out of yourself until you first repent of the hell in yourself. Many believers simply feel that they are ok, and that they are in a perfect relationship with God. Many believers are out of step but they don't realize they are out of step. You won't get in step until you realize you are out of step. The bible teaches us that there is some hell in all of us.

> *Behold, I was shapen in iniquity; and in sin did my mother conceive me. (Psalm 51:5)*

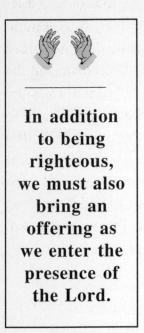

In addition to being righteous, we must also bring an offering as we enter the presence of the Lord.

Thanks be to God who gave us a cure by the way of the cross. The veil was torn. We now have access to the throne to seek His face. Like entering our computer, we cannot enter without the password. The user name is repentance and the personal P.I.N. is confession. Once we repent and confess we start our process of praising the hell out of ourselves.

In addition to being righteous, we must also bring an offering as we enter the presence of the Lord. A holy offering. II Samuel 23:15 tells of the time when David was on the run but yet doing guerrilla warfare with the Philistines. David was a great leader and he had gathered approximately four hundred men. Out of those four hundred, approximately thirty were outstanding. They were dedicated to their leader. During this period, David longed for water from the well in Bethlehem, which was under siege by the Philistines. However, he did not exercise his authority and order his men to get the water for him.

> *And David longed, and said, Oh that one would give me drink of the water of the well of Bethlehem, which is by the gate! And the three mighty men brake through the host of the*

Philistines, and drew water out of the well of Bethlehem, that was by the gate, and took it, and brought it to David: nevertheless he would not drink thereof, but poured it out unto the LORD. (II Samuel 23:15-16)

Three of the thirty chosen followers knew that their leader wanted a drink from the well at Bethlehem. They took it upon themselves to break through the enemy line of the Philistines just to get a drink of water for their leader. Upon bringing the water back to David, the scriptures tell us that David took the water and did a strange thing that, at first glance, is difficult to understand. David, after longing for the water, having thirsted for some water from home, took the water and poured it out on the ground. The scripture says that he poured it out unto the Lord. David realized that these men had risked their lives to get this water. Therefore, he sacrificed it unto the Lord. He poured it out as a holy offering.

In the book of Leviticus, we find that the tithe is Holy unto the Lord. And all the tithe of the land, whether of the seed of the land, or of the fruit of the tree, is the LORD's: it is holy unto the LORD. (Leviticus 27:30)

The question is, "What is holy unto you?" What do you desire to keep and are you willing to sacrifice it unto the Lord? God desires for you to bring Him a holy offering as you approach Him behind the veil. He wants you to offer Him a holy offering of righteousness. You need to pour it out as an offering unto the Lord. Bring an offering that means something to you. What can you bring Him? Is your time holy to you?

Would you rather spend your time doing what matters to you rather than giving it to be used for God's glory and purpose? Is your job holy to you? Do you spend more time chasing dollars rather than sitting at the feet of God? Whatever is holy unto you needs to be poured out unto the Lord.

I believe that one of the reasons pride is one of the seven deadly sins is because it blocks praise.

Football was once holy to me. I seriously doubt if I could tell you whose playing now. My wife knows that we used to sit in church and I'd be watching the time. The preacher had to hurry up and get through. I had to see the game! Football was holy to me so I had to pour it out. My 1973 El Dorado with a cabaret roof was holy to me. I had to pour it out. Now I'll drive anything anybody will give or sell me cheap. I had to pour out my prideful taste.

My jazz collection was once holy to me. I had Charlie Parker, MJQ, Miles Davis, Yardbird and others, but I had to pour them out. What's holy to you? My house at 1702 Van Aken Boulevard in Shaker Heights, Ohio was holy to me. I used to sit there and play Lou Rawls records and feel good because I thought I had a "piece of the American pie." But I had to pour it out. Is pride holy to you? If so, you cannot bring God a righteous offering. I believe that one of the reasons pride is one of the seven deadly sins is because it blocks praise.

These six things doth the LORD hate: yea, seven are an abomination unto him: A proud look, a lying tongue, and hands that shed innocent blood, An heart that deviseth wicked imaginations, feet that be swift in running to mischief, A false witness that speaketh lies, and he that soweth discord among brethren. (Proverbs 6:16-19)

Being puffed up about who you are (or think you are) is pride. It needs to be poured out.

If you need a breakthrough in your life, you may need God to breakdown the high places of pride erected in your heart.

There is a big difference between seeking God's hand and seeking His face.

Some have said that praise is a cultural thing. Praise is not cultural. That's one of the crutches that the devil has deployed against the church. Go to any Black, Hispanic or White church that has been set free to praise God. You will quickly recognize that it has nothing to do with culture. It has more to do with pride. Somehow or another, men and women find it difficult to experience the hell shattering presence of God because the hell building power of pride is so evident in their lives.

Practicing a lifestyle of pride separates a person from God, thereby nullifying their right-standing with Him. If you need a **breakthrough** in your life, you may need God to **breakdown** the high places of pride erected in your heart. Then, and only then, will you be able to give God the type of righteous offering He desires.

Far too often, Christians come to the church seeking God's hand rather than His face. Many come to church with a "give me" attitude rather than a "giving" attitude. We come asking God to give me this and give me that. He's God — not some fictitious Santa Claus with goodies for all the good little girls

and boys! I believe this type of attitude insults God and reflects the immaturity of the believer. When the high priest
went behind the veil into the Holy of Holies, **He always took
an offering!**

Why is it that we think we can go behind the veil empty-
handed and require something of the Master. There is a big
difference between seeking God's hand and seeking His face.
If you sincerely desire to bring God a righteous offering and
seek His face, the need-meeting rewards in His hand will be
available also. Which do you desire
more, the presence of God or the provisions of God? Think about it.

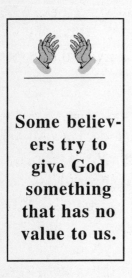

**Some believ-
ers try to
give God
something
that has no
value to us.**

Children, particularly teenagers, are
happy to see their parents because more
often than not, they are seeking what the
parents can provide. If you're honest and
will think back to your teenage days, you
were probably not much different from
me. My daddy didn't have much, and I
just wanted five dollars to get some gas
at the local store so I could see my girl-
friend. I was seeking his hand rather
than his presence. My father was 93 years old at the time of
this writing, and when I meet him, I'm just glad to see him.
Some of us need to grow up and simply recognize the blessing of being in the presence of the One who is greater than
Himself - Abba, Father!

Worship is God's party. It's His praise party. When you
go to a party, you ought to present the guest of honor with a
gift. You can't bring him any old present. You've got to
bring him a present of righteousness. You've got to bring him
something that's important to you. You wouldn't give some-

one you love something that had no meaning to you. Too often we come to parties given by people we don't care that much about. We look around in our house to see if we've got something that somebody gave us that we don't want.

Some believers try to give God something that has no value to us. If that's not bad enough, some of us who think we're "maturing in Christ" try impressing others by bringing ourselves - wrapped up in pretty boxes - with ornaments on us, as if we were gifts. God is not impressed by our outward appearance of praise and worship. He looks beyond our $600 suits and $90 hats and sees the vanity and emptiness of our hearts! Don't try to dress up to make yourself righteous. After all, our righteousness is as filthy rags in the sight of God.

Unright-eousness can never enjoy praise.

But we are all as an unclean thing, and all our righteousness are as filthy rags; and we all do fade as a leaf; and our iniquities, like the wind, have taken us away.
(Isaiah 64:6)

However, we are to:

A...present your bodies a living sacrifice, holy, acceptable unto God, which is your reasonable worship *(Romans 12:1 - NIV)*

Conclusions

First, unrighteousness can never enjoy praise. Christians who are still leaning on their own understanding (walking too much in the flesh) will never enjoy praise the way it was intended. As a point of clarification, when the bible uses the term flesh, it is not just talking about sex. It is also talking about your desirous and unrighteousness appetites; such as, leaning to your own understanding. If we lean on our own understanding, the flesh is doing whatever we desire.

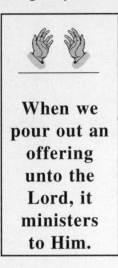

When we pour out an offering unto the Lord, it ministers to Him.

Christians who are saved, but who are not practicing walking in the Spirit, will have very little patience, especially when it comes to the area of praise and worship. To these Christians, praise may be acceptable but not enjoyable. Too often, these Christians believe that it just doesn't take all that! Those who are led by the Spirit and are walking by the Spirit, will daily seek to starve the flesh and feed the Spirit. Entering God's presence with a holy, righteous offering will not only bless God, but will also cause the Spirit of the one making the offering to be fed.

Second, when we pour out an offering unto the Lord, it ministers to Him. How can I minister to God? Who am I? How can the unholy one minister to the Holy One? If you lean to your own understanding, the answer, to the above questions will be impossible to achieve. But yet the Word of God tells us that we minister to God when we worship Him. In Exodus 29:44, you will find these words:

"And I will sanctify the tabernacle of the congregation, and the altar: I will sanctify also both Aaron and his sons, to minister to me in the priest's office."

Then in II Chronicles 29:11:

'My sons, be not now negligent: for the LORD hath chosen you to stand before him, to serve him, and that ye should

minister unto him, and burn incense."

Additionally, Acts 13:2 says of the prophets and teachers, *"As they ministered to the Lord..."*

Jesus died on the cross not only for our salvation, but also that we might worship the living God.

The bible goes on to tell us in various passages that angels can also minister to God. How awesome to know that Almighty God would allow us the privilege of ministering to Him as we adore Him! It doesn't matter who you are or what you've done, God will allow you to minister to Him. If, however, you lean to your own understanding, you will not be able to comprehend why some Christians are so extravagant in their offerings unto the Father. After all, even the disciples could not understand why Mary poured expensive perfume on Jesus and cleaned his feet with her hair. As precious as the ointment was, Mary recognized that Jesus was priceless!

Third, Jesus died on the cross not only for our salvation, but also that we might worship the living God. Why else was the veil torn? God wanted us to have direct access to Him through the great High Priest, Jesus the Christ. No longer was the blood of animals or the title of man needed to provide us access.

Once and for all, the supreme sacrifice of righteousness was paid, allowing "whosoever will" to come and present their offering unto the Lord. As Christians, we should strive to pour out those things that are righteous and holy to us. If we would place them in God's hands, then our hands would be free to worship the Provider of those things. Coming into God's presence with anything less than a holy righteous offering is totally unacceptable. God is holy and He demands and deserves our best. According to John 3:16, He gave us an example of giving a righteous offering.

> *"For God so loved the world, that he **gave***
> *his only begotten Son, that whosoever believeth*
> *in him should not perish, but have everlasting life."*
> *What do you have to offer the Lord?*

Skull Practice
Chapter Four -- Praising the Hell Out of Yourself
With Righteousness and a Holy Offering

1. How are we made right with God?
The Bible teaches that our faith makes us right with God.

2. What is necessary before we can be made right through faith?
Repentance and confession.

3. When Jesus died on the cross, why was the veil back at the Temple torn?
So that we might worship Him and have direct ac cess to Him through the great High Priest, Jesus the Christ.

4. What is the supreme and greatest example of giving a righteous offering?
John 3:16, For God so loved the world, that he gave his only begotten Son, that whosoever believeth in him should not perish, but have everlasting life.

Fill in the blanks

1. Praise cannot be effectively administered and received by God without _____. (righteousness)

2. You cannot enter into God's presence with _____. (unrighteousness)

3. Before we can be made _____, we must first repent and confess our wrong. (right)

4. In addition to being _____, we must bring a holy offering unto the Lord. (righteous)

5. _____ can never enjoy praise. (Unrighteousness)

What will be the outcome of ignoring the teaching in this chapter?

1. You never truly experience entering into His presence in worship.

2. You run the risk of being in bondage to the spirit of greed.

3. You run the risk of falling victim to one of the seven deadly sins -- pride.

4. You run the risk of never enjoying going to church.

5. You lose the opportunity to minister to God.

Helpful dialogue

1. Discuss the author's statement, "The closer you get to
    the face of God, the more you recognize the hell that
    needs to be praised out of your life."

2. Discuss the author's assertion that you cannot praise the
    hell out of yourself until you first repent the hell out of
    yourself.

3. What is the significance of David pouring out the water
    in the Lord as indicated in 2 Samuel 23:15-16.

4. According to the examples given by the author relative
    to what was holy unto Him, discuss what is meant by
    "holy unto you."

Chapter Five
Praising the Hell Out of Yourself
With Singing and Music

"I will sing unto the Lord, because he hath dealt bountifully with me." Psalm 13:6

Singing is the most supreme form of praise. Singing about and to God is a superior form of praise.

God created music for the express purpose of honoring and worshiping Him.

Music and singing is one of God's primary means to praise and worship Him. Music and singing allow our hearts and spirits to express, in a powerful way, our love for God. Earlier in this book, we talked about praising the hell out of yourself through the dance. Although the dance may be the most liberating form of praise, singing is the most supreme form of praise.

Singing about and to God is a superior form of praise. It touches our three-fold nature. It touches all of us and it touches all of our inner parts. It touches our body, spirit and soul. The spirit gets happy and the body can't stay still. When the rhythm begins to vibrate, often our hands begin to clap and our feet begin to pat. Something starts moving on the inside and we feel good. Whatever it is that causes us to move on the inside will eventually cause some movement on the outside of the body.

God created music for the express purpose of honoring and worshiping Him. Music and singing pre-date mankind. Singing is eternal. Job 38:1-7 bears witness to this fact.

"Then the LORD answered Job out of the whirlwind, and said, Who is this that darkeneth counsel by words without knowledge? Gird up now thy loins like a man; for I will demand of thee, and answer thou me. Where wast thou when I laid the foundations of the earth? declare, if thou hast understanding. Who hath laid the measures thereof, if thou knowest? or who laid the corner stone thereof; When the morning starts sang together, and all the sons of God shouted for joy?"

In this passage, God begins to ask Job a series of questions to help him remember who he was talking to. In essence, God was saying, **"I AM** God! The end was already finished before you got here! Even the stars I hung sung unto me!"

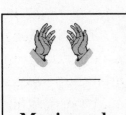

Music and singing pre-date the creation of man and will be around throughout eternity - forever.

Music and singing pre-date the creation of man and will be around throughout eternity - forever. How long is forever? Forever is forever. It's past the twelfth of never. It's eternal. At some point in the future, preaching and bible study will be over, but singing will never end. Why not make an investment in something that will serve you throughout eternity. Every opportunity you have, you should practice.

Let's talk a few moments about some of the things we do that are so temporal. You could probably mention any number of things you do on a daily basis which have little or no eternal value. Even though going to school is important, it

Practicing singing on this side of eternity may certainly help prepare you for what I believe will be a noisy, joyous eternity.

has no eternal value. Money is necessary, but not eternal. Careers are good, but not eternal. Every Christian should build their hopes on things eternal.

Singing is a good investment because it will be here forever. Every person has an eternal destiny. Everyone will spend eternity somewhere with a consciousness. The question is where? In hell, there will be crying, gnashing of teeth and continual torment. In heaven, there will be singing and worshiping. Practicing singing on this side of eternity may certainly help prepare you for what I believe will be a noisy, joyous eternity.

The Psalmist said that he would sing unto the Lord because He has dealt bountifully with him (Psalm 13:6). Singing overflows from a spirit that is happy with its Maker. When you reflect on the God-given bounty in your own life, the Spirit of God in you will cause you to create a song, because nothing else seems adequate enough to express your joy.

If you sing or hum a tune long enough, it gets stuck in your

Singing and music are an important part of the church.

head. Before long, you'll find yourself singing it and others around you will start humming it as well. There's something about music and singing that touches us at the very core of our beings.

Singing and music are an important part of the church. It prepares the heart to receive the Word of God. We must not; however, allow the choir (or music department) to hold the worship celebration in bondage.

It's ludicrous to believe that you must have a choir or musician in order to have a joyous musical experience in church. In its most fundamental state, the **congregation** is the choir, and their **voices** are the ten-stringed instruments that should be lifted up to God. I love to sing and I don't need a choir or piano in order to do it.

Sometimes we place far too much attention on having the **right** robe, the **right** type of organ, or the **right** hand clapping action and we totally miss the thrill of singing unto the Lord from a pure and holy heart. I appreciate those who serve in music ministries. However, the One to whom we are singing and making melody should always remain the focus. Additionally, the congregation should be encouraged to be participants, rather than spectators.

I am familiar with a fast growing church that believes that when they see somebody in the congregation not singing, they assume they are lost, and immediately begin to pray for them. Personally, I don't believe lost people can really praise. I don't believe an unbeliever can praise, because praise acknowledges who God is.

If you acknowledge who He is, that He is Lord, then you're not lost. If you can't give Him any praise, you might either be lost, or you just don't know Him. God has done great things in our lives. We should not be ashamed of singing aloud unto Him for His marvelous works.

God Sings

In the Old Testament, the Prophet Zephaniah gives us an encouraging thought:

"The LORD thy God in the midst of thee is mighty; he will save,
he will rejoice over thee with joy; he will rest in his love,
he will joy over thee with singing." Zephaniah 3:17

Isn't it refreshing to know that God sings? The strong and mighty Father rejoices with joy as He sings over us. The text suggests that when we are pleasing in His sight, we make God so happy that He sings. Can you imagine it? When somebody joins the church, He sings. When Christians love one another, He sings. When somebody gives their life to Him, He sings. When we take a stand for righteousness, He sings. When we praise the hell out of ourselves, God sings! What an awesome thought! If God will sing when we are pleasing to Him, how much more often should we be singing unto Him because of His bountifulness towards us.

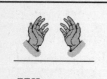

When we praise the hell out of ourselves, God sings!

The Silence of the Lambs

I believe there are a couple of reasons why we don't sing unto the Lord as we should. First, and one of the most disturbingly subtle reasons is that the devil has tricked and deceived us into believing that only the talented and trained can sing. That is a lie straight from the chief liar himself. You need to stamp that lie "Return to sender" and send it back to the pit of hell from where it originated. The same mechanisms in which you use to talk are the same ones you use when you sing. The voice is controlled by muscles, which can be trained. I'm not saying that you may want to quit your day job and start singing for a living! Even though you can sing, you may not be able pay the bills singing.

God never said to make a beautiful melody to Him. He said to make a joyful noise.

> *"Make a joyful noise unto the LORD, all ye lands"*
> *(Psalm 100:1)*

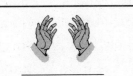

For too long, the devil has influenced us to believe that only the talented and trained should be in the choir and making melody unto God.

This means, you may not be able to understand it yourself. But if you sing unto the Lord, I believe He will receive your song as a sweet melody in His ears! For too long, the devil has influenced us to believe that only the talented and trained should be in the choir and making melody unto God. As mentioned earlier, that's part of the reason the congregation has a spectator's mentality rather than a participant's mentality.

I would venture to say that only 20% of the congregation, including the choir, are what most of us would consider singers. Also, there may be another 40% who are what I call timid contributors. They hardly open their mouths and you can barely hear any words flowing from them. So what happens to the other 40%? Do they just sit there like a bump on a log and watch other folks? Unfortunately, the answer to that question, too often, is yes. The bible commands us,

> *"Praise ye the LORD. Sing unto the LORD a new song, and his praise in the congregation of saints."*
> *(Psalm 149:1)*

The deceptive lie of the devil has stopped many of us from *praising the hell out of ourselves* through song. Some churches hold auditions for people to sing in the choir. That's simply outrageous! God did not say let the choir sing. He said all of us ought to sing. Churches should be singing congregations. Believers need to sing.

If God saved you, then He has put a new song is your heart. Don't let the devil trick you any longer! Let your song ring out in joyful praise unto God. Come into His presence with singing!

There's a second problem relative to why we don't sing unto the Lord as we should. Many still think the veil is there separating us from God. Some still think God is a God who sits high and never looks low. How could a God who is so great and so high allow me to come into His presence with my little weak voice? I find it interesting that when people **think** things are high, they determine that it is out of their reach.

Sometimes people will see me in the grocery store and be amazed. For some reason, they think that since I am a pastor of a large congregation that I am "untouchable". Often our minds are the very things that have made people and things unapproachable or untouchable.

As mentioned throughout this book, **the veil has been torn. You have direct access to the mercy seat because of Jesus Christ. Sing your song. God is waiting to hear it!**

Conclusions

1. <u>Music unifies</u>. We come into God's house, from various places and walks of life. It doesn't matter who you work for or your station in life; when the call to worship comes, we should all join in joyful praise and adoration unto the God of our salvation. Although we are many, music unifies us and makes us one voice unto God.

2. <u>God can pronounce judgement and where He does, there is no singing.</u> The Lord inhabits the praises of His people. God lives in praise. Praise gives Him home court advantage. He desires praise. But where He places His judgement, he cuts off the music. Note the following:

Praise gives Him home court advantage.

By the rivers of Babylon, there we sat down, yea, we wept, when we remembered Zion. We hanged our harps upon the willows in the midst thereof. For there they carried us away captive required of us a song; and they that wasted us required of us mirth, saying, Sing us one of the songs of Zion. How shall we sing the LORD'S song in a strange land?
(Psalm 137:1-4)

God punished the children of Israel for their sins. They had to hang their harps on the willows because they could not sing the Lord's song in the strange land they had been taken captive. Many of our churches have been taken captive, and the praises have been shut up because of unconfessed "sin in the house." We cannot sing unto the Lord with a voice of triumph because sin has snuffed out the victory in our lives. We need to clean house! Tear down the high place and build altars of singing and worship. I am very concerned about churches that are not singing churches.

Again, look at what the bible says, *"And after these things I saw another angel come down from heaven, having great power; and the earth was lightened with his glory. And he cried mightily with a strong voice, saying, Babylon the great is fallen, and is become the habitation of devils, and the hold of every foul spirit, and a cage of every unclean and hateful bird...And a mighty angel took up a stone like a great millstone, and cast it into the sea, saying, Thus with violence*

shall that great city Babylon be thrown down, and shall be
found no more at all. And the voice of harpers, and musi-
cians, and of pipers, and trumpeters, shall be found any more
in thee..." Revelation 18:1-2, 21-22.*

Also, *"Hear ye this word which I take up against you, even
a lamentation, O house of Israel...Take thou away from me
the noise of thy songs; for I will not hear the melody of thy
viols." Amos 5:1, 23.*

Based on these and other similar scriptures, I have one
simple word of caution for churches that prohibit or pervert
praise, **don't do it!** Nothing is worth risking the absence of
the presence of God in your congregation. In fact, should
you elect not to praise God any longer, **or try to praise Him
according to your agenda or bulletin**, you run the risk of
having *"Ichabod" (the glory of the Lord has departed. I
Samuel 4:21)*, written across the front door post of your
church.

Instead of the death angel passing you by, as he did during
the pre-exodus of the children of Israel from Egypt (Exodus
12:13); by shutting up and off praise, you have invited the
death angel to come in and make himself at home while the
glory of the Lord passes you by!

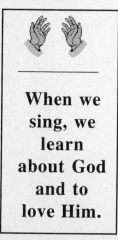

**When we
sing, we
learn
about God
and to
love Him.**

3.   <u>Singing teaches us about God.</u>
When we sing, we learn about God and to
love Him. Love is not a one time action.
When we learn to love God we will do a
lot better. Love is a process. I love my
wife more today than I did thirty-nine years
ago when I married her. The time we've
spent together has caused my love for her
to grow. I know her better and love her

more because of it. In the same manner, we can learn to love God by spending more time with Him, and by singing love songs to Him.

4. <u>Godly music is an overflow of the Christian journey</u>. God has been so good to us we need to release it in song. Have you ever been in church and a song gets in your heart? When you get home, you recognize that you're still singing that same song. Chances are that you're going to be singing that song for a while because it is a testimony of the goodness of God in your life. Sometimes you may not even know all of the words. But you simply must sing.

5. <u>When we sing, we get a spiritual foot washing.</u> In ancient bible days, foot washing was one thing people did for one another. Usually a servant or slave would have this responsibility. Because the people wore sandals and walked the dusty roads of Palestine, their feet would show the evidence of their travel. Whether you know it or not, we're living in a dusty dirty world. Everywhere we step, there is filth and sin. Some of us work on jobs that are filthy with prejudice and immorality. Some of us live in houses that are dirty with adultery or fornication. Singing has such a way of causing the body to move that your feet may get to dancing and before you know it, the presence of the Lord has flooded the place you're in and given you a complete foot washing. In fact, God's presence is so awesome that it doesn't just stop with your feet. It brings about cleansing from the top to the bottom and from the inside out! We can praise the dirt off of ourselves.

When you sing the Lord's song, your "honey" becomes Jesus, the One who will never leave you nor forsake you.

6. <u>Singing allows us to express our most intimate feelings to God.</u> Through singing, we can express our most intimate, close, and loving feelings. This is especially true with gospel and praise music. The "blues" and gospel music have some similarities. The major difference is who you're singing to. When you sing the blues, you're often singing about or to your human lover (honey) that left you. The blues will make you blue!

But when you sing the Lord's song, your "honey" becomes Jesus, the One who will never leave you nor forsake you. Hallelujah! Sing unto the Lord! Shout the praises of your Redeemer! As you enter the presence of God with singing, your soul will be revived and lifted. God delights in your sincere offering of music and singing. Don't allow another opportunity to enter through the veil with song pass you by. Try it. You may just end up *praising the hell out of yourself!*

Skull Practice
Chapter Five -- Praising the Hell Out of
Yourself With Singing and Music

1. Is singing eternal?
> Yes! Music was in the beginning and will be with us
> forever. (See Job 38:1-7)

**2.   Must believers have a gift or talent for singing before
their singing is pleasing to God?**
> *No! God said make a joyful noise, not a beautiful noise.*

3. Is singing a commandment?
> *Yes! God invites us into His presence with a definite
> command to "come into His presence with singing."*

4. Is singing important to the church?
> *As it prepares us to receive the cleansing word, it is
> God's superior mode of chasing the hell out of the be-
> liever and the church.*

5. Should singing be delegated or relegated?
> *No! Singing should encourage the entire congregation
> to be participants rather than spectators in worship.*

Fill in the blanks

1. _____ is the most supreme form of praise. (Singing)

2. _____ about and to God is a superior form of praise. (Singing)

3. Music and _____ are God's primary means to praise and worship Him. (singing)

4. Music and _____ predate the creation of man and will be around throughout eternity. (singing)

5. Bible study will be over one day, but _____ will never end. (singing)

What will be the outcome of ignoring the teaching in this chapter?

1. You run the risk of having an "I-chabod experience." (The glory of the Lord has departed. 1 Samuel 4:21)

2. You will not fully enjoy the Christian journey.

3. You will miss out on the most convenient way of making love to God.

4. You will probably never feel totally unified with the body of Christ.

5. You miss an opportunity to grow in your knowledge and love for God.

Helpful dialogue

1. Discuss two of the reasons the author feels that congregations and believers do not sing.

2. Explain what is meant by the statement, "Singing is the most user-friendly form of praise.

3. Discuss and biblically verify the awesome thought that God sings when we please Him.

4. Discuss what is meant by Apraise gives God home court advantage."

5. Cite and discuss a biblical example of when God places His judgement, music is cut off.

Chapter Six
Praising the Hell Out of Yourself
With the Tithe

*Bring all the tithes into the storehouse, that there may be
food in My house, And try Me now in this, says the Lord
of hosts, If I will not open for you the windows of heaven
and pour out for you such blessing that there will not be
room enough to receive it. And I will rebuke the
devourer for your sakes, so that he will not
destroy the fruit of your ground, nor shall the
vine fail to bear fruit for you in the field, says
the Lord of hosts   Malachi 3:10-11*

We have said that praise and worship are interrelated with some differences between the two. One of the differ-

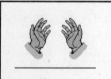

God will interact with (and on our be-half) when we worship Him through the giving of tithe.

ences is that praise can be a one-way street but worship is always a two-way communication. In other words, when we worship God, God has to play a part in it. We can give Him praise; however, we cannot give Him worship.

All of the previous chapters have talked about different methods or conditions we could use to enter into the presence of God and praise the hell out of our lives. Each method or condition was predicated upon our involvement.

Our next method of entering the presence of God is through tithing.

Tithing is an authentic act that meets both the definitions of praise and worship. As our chapter scripture indicates, God will interact with (and on our behalf) when we worship Him through the giving of tithe. God invites all that will obey to prove him. To paraphrase, God is saying, "Try me. Prove me. Test me. See what I'll do for you if you are obedient to Me in this regard. Honor Me through the tithe and watch hellish conditions be praised right our of your life!"

Just for the record, a tithe is a tenth of one's increase given in support of God's work through the church. Whether your increase is money, livestock, or time, the church (God's earthly steward) should be given the first tenth to be used for God's work. Although we will focus our discussion on praising God through the giving of a monetary tithe, it must be emphasized that tithing involves giving a tenth of **all** of your increase.

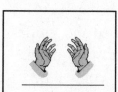

God has promised us that if we praise and worship Him through the tithe, He would rebuke the devourer from our resources.

Since God gives each of us twenty-four (24) hours in every day, a **minimum** of 2.4 hours *(daily)* should be invested in God's work in a spirit of praise and worship. Some believe that if you are a gardener, a tenth of your produce should be offered to the church to minister to the necessities of the needy. The point is, it doesn't matter whether we are talking about time, tomatoes or tender, crisp dollar bills, it all belongs to God and he simply commands us to give 10% to His work.

The most important point relative to the theme of this book is that God has promised us that if we praise and worship Him through the tithe, **He** would rebuke the devourer from our resources. Hallelujah! (Malachi 3:11) In other words, tithing fights evil. The tithe is a weapon given to saints to be used in spiritual warfare.

Notice the emphasis is placed on giving God's tithe to the church. God has always purposed His work to be done through the church as she acts as His resource steward. This simply means that you cannot tithe to the United Negro College Fund. The UNCF is a great organization that provides a needed service.

I, as well as the church I pastor, regularly contribute to the United Way or the Heart Society. However, it is a contribution and not a tithe. **GOD SAID** to bring **HIM** all of **HIS** tithes into **HIS** house. He established the guideline and command for His tithe. All of those organizations are wonderful and I encourage you to contribute to them. However, God commanded that the tithe be given to **the church** for the continuance of His work.

From a financial perspective, the tithe is the income given to the work of God in the church. In Genesis 14:18-20, we first read about tithing:

> *Then Melchizedek king of Salem brought out bread and wine; he was the priest of God most High. And he blessed him and said: "Blessed be Abram of God Most High, Possessor of heaven and earth; And blessed be God Most high, who has delivered your enemies into your hand." And he gave him a tithe of all.*

In the above passages, we see that Abraham paid a tithe to Melchizedek after God had given him the victory over the enemy. In other words, Abraham took one tenth of the spoils he received and gave it to Melchizedek as a tithe. The giving of the tithe to Melchizedek is consistent with God's command that the tithe be given to the church as His steward. We can understand this by looking at what it says in Hebrews 7:1-3.

For this Melchizedek, king of Salem, priest of the Most High God, who met Abraham returning from the slaughter of the kings and blessed him, to whom also Abraham gave a tenth part of all, first being translated "king of righteousness," and then also "king of peace," without father, without mother, without genealogy, having neither beginning of days nor end of life, but made like the Son of God, remains a priest continually.

Since then Melchizedek is a type of Christ, and Christ is the head of the church, scripture confirms itself in Abraham's form of praise unto God through the tithe.

Since then Melchizedek is a type of Christ, and Christ is the head of the church, scripture confirms itself in Abraham's form of praise unto God through the tithe.

I personally find it interesting that Abraham was coming out of Africa, the birthplace and cradle of civilization, when he met Melchizedek. It may have been there where Abraham learned how to praise the hell out of his life.

Think about it. He had to learn this method of worship from somewhere! Isn't it an awesome thought that Abraham, this great man of faith, may have learned tithing from Africans. To understand the

As Christians, we can't possibly think we can favorably enter God's presence bringing Him our leftovers!"

If we believe God as it relates to our giving, we will drop our tithe envelopes in the offering plates and *praise the hell out of ourselves* all the way back to our seats, knowing that God promised to rebuke the devourer for our sakes!

significance of this, we must further explore Hebrews 7:1-3.

Abraham, who paid the tithe, is known as the Father of Faith. The bible tells us that a good steward is found faithful and without faith it is impossible to please God. Anything we can reason and apply logic to cannot be called faith. If you can see it or count it, it cannot be called faith. You've got to get out on a limb to have and operate in faith. Herein lies one reason why we won't praise and worship God through the giving of tithe.

Faith requires that you go out on a limb! What does that mean as it relates to our giving? Simply put, God did not say praise me through the tithe only if you have enough money for everything else you want! He said, "prove me! Have faith in Me and I'll take care of your devouring enemy!

As Christians, we can't possibly think we can favorably enter God's presence bringing Him our leftovers!" We've got to believe that God will supply our every "daily bread."

If we believe God as it relates to our giving, we will drop our tithe envelopes in the offering plates and *praise the hell out of ourselves* all the way back to our seats, knowing that God **promised** to rebuke the devourer for our sakes! That's awesome!

Tithing is an Issue of Faith

How and whether we give our money to God speaks loudly of the amount of faith we have in Him. Tithing, like every other form of praise and worship must be entered into in faith. *But without faith it is impossible to please him: for he that cometh to* God **must believe that He is**, and that He is a rewarder of them *that diligently seek Him. (bold added)*

The question is to believe that He is? When you bring the tithe to the house of God and offer it to Him, do you **really believe** that you are giving it to the One who really is God? By faith, do you believe that He will use it for His glory for the work of His kingdom?

Do you really believe that He will rebuke the devourer for your sake, even though it appears that you have more month than money? If so, then your faith should cause you to give cheerfully and praise loudly! But you must believe.

Through many acts of faith and faithfulness, Abraham earned an outstanding title. God gave him the title Father of Faith. Who can forget the mighty act of faith Abraham displayed when he took his only son to the top of Mt. Moriah and prepared to sacrificially kill and offer him to God? Because God had given Abraham His word that He was going to make him a father of many nations, Abraham had much faith that God would, if necessary, resurrect the boy just to fulfill His promise! That's faith!

What about your children? Will you sacrifice them to God? I have three children, and I don't believe I would give either of them in the manner Abraham was to sacrifice his son, Isaac. If we believe as Abraham did that God has the ability to resurrect even to keep a promise, how much more should we believe Him to keep His promise regarding tithing?

Tithing Means Worshiping in Spirit and Truth

In addition to faithfulness, another problem we Christians face when it comes to praising the hell out of ourselves through the giving of tithes is we want to worship God in spirit, but not in truth. The bible clearly states that we are to worship Him in both spirit and truth.

> *But the hour cometh, and now is, when*
> *the true worshiper shall worship the*
> *Father in spirit and truth: for the*
> *Father seeketh such to worship Him.*
> *John 4:23*

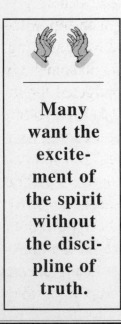

Many want the excitement of the spirit without the discipline of truth.

There's a strange and foundationally demonic movement sweeping the Church today. Some folks have gotten so *"spiritually minded"* that they are no *"earthly good."* In other words, we want to dance in the spirit, but not live by His word. Many want the excitement of the spirit without the discipline of truth. To succumb to this type of thinking and action is absolutely ridiculous since Christ Himself called the Holy Spirit the Spirit of Truth! (John 16:13)

Let me ask the following question. Does the teaching and preaching on money make you a little uncomfortable? If so, this may be an indication that there is some hell in you that needs to come out. The first thing to recognize is that it is not your money. It all belongs to God. He simply asked for one tenth.

We should praise Him for not asking for the 90%, leaving us with only 10%! The bottom line is that God commanded that we bring Him the tithe. It doesn't even matter whether or not the preacher is stealing the money. You ought to tithe one way, or find a church in which you're comfortable. Your sin of disobedience in not tithing is just as wrong as a preacher's sin of stealing. In a very real sense, they are basically the same. Both the non-tithing believer and the stealing preacher are robbers in the sight of God! So what is the relationship between praise and tithing? Note these spiritual truths.

You cannot worship without giving.

1.   Worship and giving are inseparable. You cannot worship without giving. **It is impossible to worship without giving.** The first year I was pastoring, we budgeted for a revival and somebody asked me how is it we budgeted for revival and we still planned to lift an offering. The reason is that you cannot have revival without worshiping God and you cannot worship God without giving. You cannot budget that. You may budget for the honorarium and those sorts of things, but you cannot worship without giving. The two are inseparable. Throughout biblical history, it doesn't matter whether it was Jacob, Abraham, Malachi, Moses, the wise men or Christ, they

worship by giving an offering unto God. I find it interesting that oftentimes, when I go to visit various churches, I almost have to get up and take my gift because no one comes to bring the plate to the guest preacher.

In fact, I was in one church and they did not even pass the offering plate in the choir. It was as if the preacher and the choir were exempt from worshiping God when in actuality, they should be the leaders in worship. After all, each of us should follow the supreme example of giving.

*For God so loved the world that **He gave**... (bold added)*

2. Tithing is an act of worship because it puts us in right relationship with God. If you are not a worshiper, you are not in perfect relationship with God. Therefore, if you are not a tither, you are not in perfect relationship with God. To be a non-tither is disobedience and disobedience is sin. Just as sure as "co-habitating" (shacking up) is a sin, so is withholding God's tithe from the storehouse. You may not be shacking up with a person, but if you are not tithing you are shacking up with a spirit that is not of God. See if any of these names sound familiar: spirit of rebellion, spirit of greed, spirit of hoarding, spirit of stealing. Tithing will put you in right relationship

Tithing is an act of worship because it puts us in right relationship with God.

Tithing will put you in right relationship with God so that you can *praise hellish spirits right out of your life!*

with God so that you can *praise hellish spirits right out of your life!*

3. Tithing is an act of praise because it acknowledges God for who He is. You will never be in right relationship with God until you acknowledge who He is. You must acknowledge that He is the Owner. He owns you. He owns the breath that you breathe and the very essence of who you are. God owns everything and until you acknowledge that fact, you cannot properly give Him what He desires — praise through tithing. He is Creator and we are but creatures. You cannot worship Him without first praising Him.

4. Tithing pre-dates and post-dates the law. It is not a legalistic matter. When we tithe legalistically, God does not honor that anymore than He honored the Pharisee's tithe. Tithing predates the Mosaic law and the Levitical law. Tithing goes back biblically at least to Abraham and possibly to Cain and Abel. In conclusion, words taken from a book I was blessed to author entitled, *"Faithful Over a Few Things,"* are appropriate.

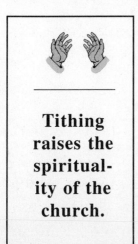

Tithing raises the spirituality of the church.

Tithing is not a matter of money. It is a matter of faith. We have tried to make it a money issue. Tithing raises the spirituality of the church. The real question is how much faith do you have? Do you have enough faith to step across the line of doubt? How far out on a limb will you go? God wants us to depend on Him. He wants us to try Him. To test Him. To ultimately prove Him.   "If you will step across the line of doubt into the area of faith, God's word promises you victory." Praising the hell out of yourself through tithing will give you this victory.

Skull Practice
Chapter Six -- Praising the Hell Out of Yourself
With The Tithe

1.   What is a tithe?
   *A Tithe is a tenth of one's increase given in sup
   port of God's work through the church.*

**2.   How do we discern that giving a tithe is a weapon to
fight evil, and praise the hell out of ourselves?**
   *Because God promised us that if we praise and
   worship Him through the tithe He "will rebuke the
   devourer for your sakes... (Malachi 3:11)*

3.   Is it possible to worship without giving?
   No!   Worship and giving are inseparable.

4.   Is it possible to please God without tithing?
   *No, because tithing is a matter of faith, and it is
   impossible to please God without faith.*
   (Hebrews 11:6)

Fill in the blanks

1. God will interact with (and on our behalf) when we
   worship Him through the giving of
   _____. (tithes)

2. _____ is an authentic act that meets
   both the definitions of praise and worship. (Tithing)

3. The _____ is yet another weapon given to the saints to be used in spiritual warfare. (tithe)

4. _____ is an issue of faith. (Tithing)

5. _____ involves worshiping God in spirit and truth. (Tithing)

6. _____ is an act of worship because it puts us in the right relationship with God. (Tithing)

7. _____ is an act of praise because it acknowledges God for who He is. (Tithing)

What will be the outcome of ignoring the teaching in this chapter?

1. You will not be in a perfect relationship with God.

2. You will forfeit the greatest opportunity to demonstrate your love for God.

3. You will not please God.

4. You will prove to God that you neither believe Him or trust Him.

5. You forfeit the opportunity you have with God as a participating partner in your business and/or personal finances.

6. You miss out on a marvelous opportunity to praise the spirit of doubt out of yourself.

Helpful dialogue

1. Discuss how honoring God with the tithe is both praise and worship.

2. Discuss the meaning of the author's statement, "Many want the excitement of the spirit without the discipline of the truth.

3. Discuss the author's statement, "You may not be shacking up with a person, but if you are not tithing you are shacking up (cohabiting) with a spirit that is not of God.

4. Discuss the implications of tithing as an issue of faith rather than a matter of money.

5. Discuss the implications of the fact that tithing pre-dates and postdates the law.

Chapter 7
Praising the Hell Out of Yourself in Time of Trouble

"Let us therefore come boldly unto the throne of grace, that we may obtain mercy, and find grace to help in the time of need." (Hebrews 4:16)

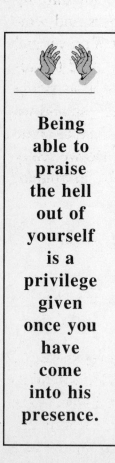

Being able to praise the hell out of yourself is a privilege given once you have come into his presence.

As stated earlier in chapter one--but it bears repeating—although we are specifically dealing with praising the hell out of yourself, we are also concerned about coming into the presence of God, with the highest aim being obedience to His word relative to praise and worship.

Being able to praise the hell out of yourself is a privilege given once you have come into his presence. As we endeavor to become people who will worship God in spirit **and truth,** the "when" of coming into His presence must be addressed in addition to the "how" of coming into His presence.

This chapter will focus on the "when" of coming into God's presence. We are taught that we can and should come into His presence in a time of trouble. Times of crises come to all of us. If you have not yet experienced one, keep living. Dr. Beecher Hicks, in his book entitled *Preaching Through the Storm* asserts that we are all in one of three positions: (1) coming into a storm, (2) in the midst of a storm, or (3) coming out of a storm.

After reading this assertion, I took inventory of my life. I realized that I was not in the midst of a storm; and that I was not coming out of a storm. Therefore, if there was any truth to the assertion, I evidently was coming into a storm.

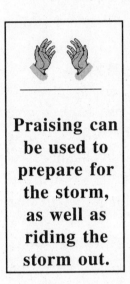

Praising can be used to prepare for the storm, as well as riding the storm out.

Therefore, I immediately began to prepare for a storm by boarding up my life with storm doors and windows, and the plywood of prayer and praise. Praising can be used to prepare for the storm, as well as riding the storm out. Why then, should we feel embarrassed or hesitant to come to the Lord when a crisis comes our way? Do we really believe that God does not already know we're in trouble! God tells us through Job that,

Yet man is born unto trouble, as the sparks fly upward.
(Job 5:7)

Man that is born of a woman is of a few days, and full of trouble. (Job 14:1)

So often, I have experienced people saying to me, "I don't want to come to the Lord now because God will think that I am only coming because I'm in trouble. I want to get my life straightened out and then I will come. I want to get my home life in order and then I'll give Him my life and

In the midst of spiritual warfare is not the time for us to apply our logic.

We spend too much time on the battlefield of spiritual warfare, thinking about how we can get out of trouble, rather than praising God in the midst of our circumstances.

maybe join the church." Far too often, we try to do God's job. We try to help Him do what only He can do! The truth is, if we could have gotten our lives together enough by just "coming to church," we probably would have by now. Often, we think too highly of our abilities. I firmly believe that there are some things that God does not want us to think or be concerned about.

Certainly, I am not referring to when you are in the office dealing with databases and spreadsheets. I am referring to when you're in the midst of crises or engaging in intense spiritual warfare.

In the midst of spiritual warfare is not the time for us to apply our logic. If we knew everything there was to know about the battle, we would not have been in it in the first place. Additionally, there would be no need for anybody to give us instruction.

God does not want us to lean to our own understanding. God says, if we just need to think, let Me tell you what to think about.

"Finally, brethren, whatsoever things are true, whatsoever things are honest, whatsoever things are just, whatsoever

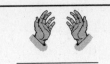

Every believer has the ability to enter through the veil, up to the mercy seat and into the very presence of Almighty God!

The devil has stolen the joy of Jesus and access behind the veil out of some of our hearts.

things are pure, whatsoever things are lovely, whatsoever things are of a good report; if there be any virtue, and if there be any praise, think on these things."
(Philippians 4:8)

We spend too much time on the battlefield of spiritual warfare, thinking about how we can get out of trouble, rather than praising God in the midst of our circumstances.

My first job, after paperboy, paid 13 cents per hour. I had the unenviable responsibility of picking up manure at a dairy, and transporting it to the manure pit. (Now you can see why I praise God so much for His delivering power!) As difficult as picking up the manure was, it was even worse when we had to clean out the manure pit and spread the manure on the garden. Because of His mercy, God promoted me and I got a construction job rolling a wheelbarrow full of cement and bricks in about 110 degree temperature. Part of the job was to roll the bricks up to the brick mason - the person laying the brick.

One day, I got a big idea about a better way to get the bricks up to the brick mason. So, I went to the boss and said to him, "I think." He

How many times, as Christians, do we begin "thinking" too hard when trouble comes our way.

stopped me right there. He said, "Hold it. Hold it. Who told you that you could think? As a matter of fact, I'm not paying you to think. What I am paying you for is to take that wheelbarrow, roll it up, and give those bricks to my brick mason."

I thought about that in relation to spiritual warfare. God is saying to us, "Who told you to try and figure this crisis out? Didn't I tell you to acknowledge Me in all your ways and I would direct your path? Didn't I tell you that **I AM** the strategist in this battle? You keep trying to figure it out so you can try to work it out without coming to Me."

How many times, as Christians, do we begin "thinking" too hard when trouble comes our way. One of the first things that will happen is that our attendance and service in church will begin to dwindle. If we're going though a divorce -- we try to figure it out.

Our children are rebelling -- we try to figure it out. We have more month than money -- we try to figure it out. Daughter comes home pregnant -- we try to figure it out. These things should not send us cowering away from the presence of God, but should send us running to the mercy seat!

Sooner or later, once you've tasted and seen that the Lord is good, you're going to have an Isaiah/Uzziah experience. Isaiah's friend, king Uzziah had died. He was in a grief crisis. In the midst of this crisis, Isaiah said that he saw the Lord. What's your "Uzziah"? What will it take for you to see the Lord high and lifted up, in a seat of power and authority, higher than your problems or circumstances?

King David had no problem going to the Lord in the time of trouble. Whenever it appeared that all hell was breaking loose around him, he went to God. Throughout his life, David was faced with many challenges. Although God had His hand upon him and David did great exploits for Him, the amount of adversity in his life would have driven most of us to the insane asylum. Just look at the following points about his life.

- Not even the Prophet Samuel expected David to be anointed king because of his size and youth.

- David was given the least desirable job of those days -- a shepherd

- He faced and defeated lions, bears and a giant.

- He won the favor of a people (Israel) but was despised by the king of the people (Saul).

- He had to live in hiding and as a fugitive even though he was innocent.

- He committed adultery, murder and subsequently suffered the loss of a child.

- One of his sons raped his own sister.

- Another son rebelled against him, and again, he was sought as a fugitive.

Need I say more. I'm sure you will agree with me that David saw many crises in his lifetime. Each time he had a need in his life, he knew where to turn for direction, protection and forgiveness. Some of David's heartfelt experiences are expressed in the 27th Psalm.

The Lord is my light and my salvation; whom shall I fear? the Lord is the strength of my life; of whom shall I be afraid? When the wicked, even mine enemies and my foes, came upon me to eat up

*my flesh, they stumbled and fell. Though an host should encamp
against me, my heart shall not fear: though war should rise
against me, in this will I be confident. One thing have I desired
of the Lord, that will I seek after; that I may dwell in the house of
the Lord all the days of my life, to behold the beauty of the Lord,
and to inquire in his temple. For in the time of trouble he shall
hide me in his pavilion: in the secret of his tabernacle shall he
hide me; he shall set me up upon a rock. And now shall mine head
be lifted up above mine enemies round about me: therefore will I
offer in his tabernacle sacrifices of joy; I will sing, yea, I will sing
praises unto the Lord. Hear, O Lord, when I cry with my voice:
have mercy also upon me, and answer me. When thou saidst, Seek
ye my face; my heart said unto thee, Thy face, Lord, will I seek.
Hide not thy face far from me; put not thy servant away in anger:
thou hast been my help; leave me not, neither forsake me, then the
Lord will take me up. Teach me thy way, O Lord, and lead me in a
plain path, because of mine enemies. Deliver me not over unto the
will of mine enemies: for false witnesses are risen up against me,
and such as breath out cruelty. I had fainted, unless I had believed
to see the goodness of the Lord in the land of the living. Wait on
the Lord: be of good courage, and he shall strengthen thine heart:
wait, I say, on the Lord.*

During one specific crisis in his life, David's father-in-law became obsessed with killing him. He wanted David dead so bad that he sent messengers to get him without taking him out of his bed! David's wife, Michal, interceded on his behalf and assisted him in his escape. David knew where to go. He retreated to the man of God, Samuel, in Ramah, where he had a university of prophets.

At the school of the prophets with Samuel, David found refuge. The scriptures said that on one occasion, Samuel and the prophets were prophesying when Saul's messengers came to kill David. I believe they were praising God since the bible speaks of prophesying with the tambourine and the harp.

I don't know the exact form of praise they were engaged in, but the Living Bible paraphrases that they were in a frenzy. Maybe they were doing a holy dance or a shabach. (Shabach is a shout. For example: repeatedly saying "Hallelujah.") Maybe they were rocking and shabaching. The bible doesn't clearly say. They may have been speaking in tongues or lifting holy hands. Whatever they were doing, the bible says that when the messengers came upon them to kill David.

The spirit of the Lord then moved upon them, and they began prophesying as well! Saul sent two additional groups to seek out David, and the same thing happened to them! Totally frustrated, Saul decided to go himself. He must have thought, "What in the world is going on in Ramah? I'll have to go myself. My messengers couldn't kill him. I'll take him down."

The bible said that King Saul, in all of his kingly attire went himself to kill David. Upon his arrival at the school of the prophets, Saul himself, pulled off his clothes and lay down day and night, giving homage and acknowledging the God they were praising. He too began to prophesy. Hallelujah!

Then went he also to Ramah, and came to a great well that
is in Sechu: and he asked and said, Where are Samuel and
David? And one said, Behold, they be at Naioth and Ramah.
And he stripped off his clothes also, and prophesied before
Samuel in like manner, and lay down naked all that day
and all that night. Wherefore they say,
Is Saul also among the prophets.
(I Samuel 19:21-24)

Intense praise will run *the hell right out of your situation!*

This passage shows us that intense praise during times of adversity can change the wrath of evil men or wicked situations. If you are experiencing a crisis on your job, put it under the conviction of prayer and praise. If someone in your home is not doing right, begin to praise. If you're in the midst of any type of crises, God wants you to praise Him! Intense praise will run *the hell right out of your situation!*

If there is hell in your church, engage in intense praise. It will run the hell completely out of the church, too. Be careful. Some members may exit with the hell! The bible says that God inhabits the praises of His people. He literally comes down and makes Himself at home in the midst of   our praise, and begins to clean house!

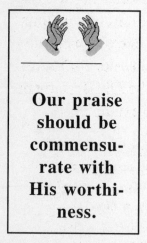

Our praise should be commensurate with His worthiness.

Our praise should be commensurate with His worthiness. Our praise should match how worthy He is. When I was teaching at Georgia State University, one of the classes I taught was in behavioral teacher training. One of the things that I would tell my students is that your feedback to your students should match the task they performed. In other words, if they did a real good job and it was a difficult task, you should say more than just "good job." But if it was a small task they performed, the response can be minimal. The feedback should match the task.

I don't know about you, but when I think of the goodness of God and all that He has done for me - the worthiness of God far exceeds my finite ability to praise Him. Much like David, when I reflect upon all the times He delivered me from the hand of my enemies, I often find my praise not "measuring up." In other words, I come short! Many church bodies are coming up short. In many instances, from the pulpit to the door, God has delivered people from alcohol, crack, homelessness, joblessness, broken heartedness, etc.

God didn't just deliver individuals, He has delivered some churches. Some congregations, specifically pastors, can remember when they didn't know how they were going to keep the lights on and the building open. They can remember when the "best tithers" got mad and left the church. They can look back and see when they had no musician and had to use a little tape recorder to provide the ministry of music. Others remember dreading to go to church because of the conflict with the deacons or trustees. Still others remember the lies told and the sheep stolen. I believe all of these crises are crying our for praise!

Praise in adversity is not limited to the Old Testament. Consider the following New Testament example.

> *"And a woman having an issue of blood twelve years,*
> *which had spent all her living upon physicians, neither*
> *could be healed of any. Came behind him, and touched*
> *the border of his garment: and immediately her issue of*
> *blood stanched. And Jesus said, Who touched me? When*
> *all denied, Peter and they that were with him said, Master,*
> *the multitude throng thee and press thee, and sayest thou,*
> *Who touched me? And Jesus said, Somebody hath touched*
> *me: for I perceive that virtue is gone out of me. And when*

the woman saw that she was not hid, she came trembling,
and falling down before him, she declared unto him before
all the people for what cause she had touched him and
how she was healed immediately. And he said unto her,
Daughter, be of good comfort: thy faith hath made thee
whole; go in peace." (Luke 8:43-48)

Now this poor woman had a 12-year long crisis. Even David had periods of rest and success during his many life crises. But this lady had a crisis for twelve straight years! As a matter of fact, she had lost her husband, spent all her money and visited every doctor in town. She was considered unclean, and had to announce her condition any time she came around people. How humiliating! She was experiencing a time of trouble, and nothing else she tried worked for her. But thanks be unto God that somebody told her Jesus was coming to her town. I can imagine somebody saying, "You've tried every doctor in town. Why don't you try the man they call Jesus. I hear He's been giving sight to the blind and causing the lame to walk. What have you got to lose? Even though you're in trouble right now, don't shy away from Him. He specializes in troubling situations!"

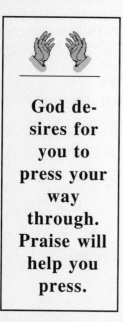

God desires for you to press your way through. Praise will help you press.

Like the woman who formally had an issue of blood, God desires for you to press your way through. Praise will help you press. None of us possess the ability to effectively pull ourselves out of the adverse situations we find ourselves in. If we could, we would; thereby making the following unnecessary,

"Let us therefore come boldly unto the throne of grace, that we may obtain mercy, and find grace to help in time of need."
(Hebrews 4:16)

God knows that we need Him. In good times as well as bad, he desires for us - his crowning creation - to press through adversity and into His very presence. Prayer and praise, the other power twins (grace and mercy are also power twins), will cause your problems to look smaller and smaller. God will become so large that you, too, will see Him high and lifted up. So look up. Start praising. Praise yourself right out of your hell, and into the presence of the only One who can work all things together for your good!

Skull Practice
Chapter Seven — Praising the Hell Out of Yourself In Time of Trouble

1. Should we only seek to come into His presence during favorable times?

No. God invites us to come into His presence during times of trouble.

2. Are believers sheltered from the storms of life?

No. Believers will be faced with crises, storms, and trouble.

3. Can believers prepare for the storms that are certain to come into their lives?

Yes, by boarding up their lives with praise and prayer.

4. Is there a remedy for believers who are already in a storm?

Yes, the remedy is praise. We can ride out and eventually overcome storms through praise.

Fill in the blanks

1. We can come into His presence in times of _____. (trouble)

2. Praise can be used to prepare for _____. (trouble)

3. Praise can be used to overcome _____. (trouble)

4. Praise can be used to endure _____. (trouble)

What will be the outcome of ignoring the teaching in this chapter?

1. You will experience too much frustration and agony in times of trouble.

2. You will run the rusk of not experiencing the fullness of the abundant life that Jesus came to bring.

3. You will not be victorious in times of trouble.

4. You run the risk of being un-Christian by fighting evil with evil rather than being obedient to the Christian teaching of overcoming evil with good.

5. You run the risk of becoming victimized by negative thinking.

Helpful dialogue

1.   Discuss the reference in this chapter to Dr. Beecher's book, *Preaching Through the Storm.*

2.   Explain the author's statement, "We spend too much time on the battlefield of spiritual warfare thinking about how we can get out of trouble, rather than praising God in the midst of our circumstances."

3.   Elaborate on your answer to the author's question, "What is your Uzziah?"

4.   Discuss the trouble and adversity that beset the life of the biblical character David. What was David's response to his trouble and adversity?

Chapter Eight
Praising the Hell Out of Yourself
with a Childlike Character

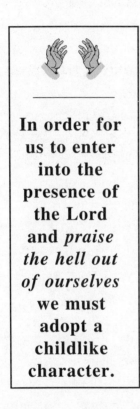

And said unto him, Hearest thou what these say? And Jesus saith unto them, Yea; have you never read, Out of the mouth of babes and sucklings thou hast perfected praise? Matthew 21:16

In order for us to enter into the presence of the Lord and *praise the hell out of ourselves* we must adopt a childlike character.

Without question, children are this world's most valuable resource. It is through the eyes and actions of children that rainbows can be seen and described. Through their ears, a symphony can be heard through a mountain stream. Through their emotions the simplest yet greatest acts of love can be displayed.

However, children possess a certain amount of purity and honesty that doesn't have to be "worked up." It's just there. This is what I call childlike character. If you have children or have been around them for a period of time, I know you know what I am talking about.

In order for us to enter into the presence of the Lord and *praise the hell out of ourselves* we must adopt a childlike character. Notice, I said "childlike" not "childish"

When I was a child, I spake as a child, I understood (felt)
as a child, I thought as a child: but when I became
*a man, I put **away childish** things.*
(Bold added for emphasis) I Corinthians 13:11

Childishness has no place in the presence of God unless you are there to repent of it! Childishness is evident by temper tantrums and lies when you don't get your way. Whining about your toy Lexus being broken instead of just driving the Acura. Childish behavior can be characterized as: rolling your eyes and your neck, and putting your hand on your hip when you're trying to make a point! Such behavior is in direct opposition to their honesty and purity of a childlike character, and must be put away in order to have an audience with the Master.

Children will come to us and make various requests. As they present their request, most parents normally ask them a series of questions such as, "Why should I get you this? What are you going to do with it. **When's the last time you cleaned your room?"**

After these and often other questions, the parent's patent answer is either, "Let me think about it" or "I'll see". *Then* childlike of childish behavior on the part of the child kicks in. Either the child will throw a temper tantrum, try one last time to persuade you to immediately give them an answer, or assume your "I'll see" to mean "yes, but later" and go away making preparation to receive the requested item.

The child who had the temper tantrum runs the very real risk of experiencing the rod of correction and a promise they will not receive the item until they are twenty-one years old! Why twenty-one? Because the parent assumes by that time, their childish behavior would have disap-

Believers with childlike character believe that their heavenly Father loves them so much that He will move heaven and earth just to make sure they are alright.

peared! God knows that as His children, we sometimes display childish behavior. His desire; however, is that we mature and display childlike character.

As children, most of us had to endure the wrath of a bully. After explaining to our parents our dilemma, we found comfort in knowing we had parental support. In similar manner, believers with childlike character believe that their heavenly Father loves them so much that He will move heaven and earth just to make sure they are alright. Just for a moment, imagine yourself cornered by your childhood bully or your modern day enemy (the devil). See with your spirit the childlike faith of the Psalmist David:

[1]I will love thee, O LORD, my strength. [2]The LORD is my rock, and my fortress, and my deliverer; my God, strength, in whom I trust; my buckler, and the horn of my salvation, and my high tower. [3]I will call upon the LORD, who is worthy to be praised: so shall I be saved from mine enemies. [4]The sorrows of death compassed me, and the floods of ungodly men made me afraid. [5]The sorrows of hell compassed me about: the snares of death prevented me. [6]In my distress, I called upon the Lord, and cried unto my God: he heard my voice out of his temple, and my cry came before him, even into his ears. **[7]Then the earth shook and trembled; the foundations also of the hills moved and were shaken, because he was wroth.** *[8]There went up a smoke out*

of his nostrils, and fire out of his mouth devoured: coals were kindled by it. ⁹He bowed the heavens also, and came down: and darkness was under his feet. ¹⁰And he rode upon a cherub, and did fly: yea, he did fly upon the wings of the wind. ¹¹He made darkness his secret place; his pavilion round about him were dark waters and thick clouds of the skies. ¹²At the brightness that was before him his thick clouds passed, hail stones and coals of fire. ¹³The LORD also thundered in the heavens, and the Highest gave his voice; hail stones and coals of fire. ¹⁴Yea, he sent out his arrows, and scattered them; and he shot out lightnings, and discomfited them. ¹⁵Then the channels of waters were seen, and the foundations of the world were discovered at thy rebuke, O LORD, at the blast of thy breath of thy nostrils. ¹⁶He sent from above, he took me, he drew me out of many waters. ¹⁷He delivered me from my strong enemy, and from them which hated me: for they were too strong for me. (Bold added for emphasis)

Psalm 18:1-17

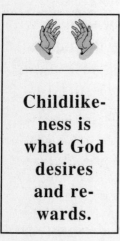

Childlike-ness is what God desires and re-wards.

Can't you see your Heavenly Father whipping up on your bully, the devil! If that won't make you praise the hell out of yourself nothing will! Childlikeness is what God desires and rewards. Once Jesus was asked who was the greatest in the kingdom of heaven (Matthew 18:1). Jesus' reply was profound.

²And Jesus called a little child unto him, and set him in the midst of them, ³And said, Verily I say unto you, Except ye be converted, and become as little children, ye shall not enter into the kingdom of heaven. ⁴Whosoever therefore

Childlikeness is a prerequisite for entrance into the kingdom of heaven as well as a key to enter into his presence in worship.

shall humble himself as this little child, the same is greatest in the kingdom of heaven.

Childlikeness is a prerequisite for entrance into the kingdom of heaven as well as a key to enter into his presence in worship.

In the scripture passage referenced at the beginning of the chapter, (Matthew 21:16) we can see another instance where childlike faith and character was encouraged by Jesus. As Jesus entered Jerusalem riding upon a donkey on the day we celebrate Palm Sunday, many laid their garments down so that he could proceed across them. As they shouted Hosanna! Hosanna!, they gave Him a royal welcome. They were excited! They were glad to see Him! They had heard of His wondrous miracles! They had heard how He had been whipping up on their bully, the devil! However adult-like hatred and wrath would soon replace this childlike display of gratitude and praise!

Probably the next day, Jesus proceeded to the temple and cleaned it by angrily ejecting the money changers and exploiters. Of course, this behavior further angered the priests and scribes who were already upset because of the people's fascination and acceptance of Christ (Matthew 21:10). This however, did not stop Jesus. As the lame and blind came to Him, He healed them. Notice what happens in the following verses.

*And when the chief priests and scribes saw the wonderful
things that he did, and **the children crying in the temple,
and saying, Hosanna to the Son of David**; they were
sore displeased, And said unto him, Hearest thou
what these say? And Jesus saith unto them, Yea; have
ye never read, Out of the mouth of babes and sucklings
thou hast perfected praise? Matthew 21:15-16*

Isn't it interesting that the adults had shut up and begun
to get angry while the children continued to praise Jesus.
They kept on saying, Hosanna to the son of David! I can
imagine the priests and scribes were so angry they instructed the children to "Be quiet", "Go somewhere and
sit down" or even better, "Get out of here. This is grown
folk's business!"

Jesus then hit them where it really hurt. To these adult
men, who thought they had it going on, who felt that they
had cornered the market on God and worship, to these same
men, Jesus told them that praise had been perfected in the
mouth of babes and sucklings! Wow! Talk about creating
a scene! Basically Jesus said, Athose who possess childlike humility and a total dependence on me, God has ordained and perfected praise in them. If you really want to
know how to *praise the hell out of yourself*, become as
dependent on God as a baby is dependent upon his parents.

Often as adults, we miss the opportunity to properly
praise and worship God because we put away childlikeness rather than childishness. We spend far too much time
looking at the people around us and being impressed with
ourselves and our accomplishments. Should it really matter to you what your neighbor thinks if you raise holy hands,

Even if you have an extremely high I.Q., how smart are you really if you can't freely praise the One who bowed the heavens and came down to see about you?

dance in the spirit, or take a victory lap around your church?

Should you really care what they think about your radical praise just because you own a successful business or hold a Ph.D.? Even if you have an extremely high I.Q., how smart are you really if you can't freely praise the One who bowed the heavens and came down to see about you? After all, with childlike fondness, you should be able to remember who showed up at your hospital bed when the doctor's had given up on you. Who caused you to have favor with the mortgage company to get that house when your credit wasn't so good?

Who whispered the answer to the question in your ear just when you thought you were about to flunk that exam? Who caused your enemy to seek your forgiveness and your friendship? Who caused that check you should have received years ago to show up the same day your lights were getting ready to be cut off?

You see, with childlike faith and gratitude, if you're not careful, you'll find yourself giving God a crazy, perfected praise that will cause you to *praise the hell right out of yourself!* Here are just a few examples of childlike behavior:

1. Joshua marching around the walls of Jericho (Joshua 6:1-5). *...and the walls came tumbling down!* A man let-

ting Jesus make mud cakes out of spit and put it on his eyes (John 9:1-7).

> *...I once was blind but now I see!*

2. Peter getting out of the safety of a boat to walk on the wave tossed sea (Matthew 14:24-33).

> *...Take a step of faith!*

3. A woman with a 12-year, incurable condition believing all she had to do was reach out and touch the Master (Matthew 9:20-22).

> *Your childlike faith has made you whole!*

4. Two expert fishermen are sent to look in the mouth of the first fish they catch for tax money (Matthew 17:27).

> *Notwithstanding, lest we should offend them, go thou to the sea, and cast a hook, and take up the fish that first cometh up; and when thou hast opened his mouth, thou shalt find a piece of money: that take and give unto them for me and thee.*

What is it about children that makes their praise so genuine before the Lord?

Children are not easily intimidated.

1. Children are not easily intimidated. Unlike children, adults are more likely to be intimidated by what others think and perceive them to be. Emotionalism may be perceived as weakness. Expressions of praise may be perceived as fanaticism. Acts of praise may be perceived as lack of intellectualism. These and other pos-

sible perceptions intimidate adults to the point that they forfeit the great weapon that God has given man for spiritual warfare, namely praise.

Children are uninhibited in their actions.

2. Children are uninhibited in their actions. Watch out! They may say anything! Children are much more uninhibited than adults. Adults have been trained through the developmental stages of life to simply be cautious in all their endeavors. In most cases, this is admired, but the downside of this positive is that it causes adults to not utilize the weapon of praise.

Children are teachable and coachable.

3. Children are teachable and coachable. Seemingly, the older we become, the less receptive we become to learning. Children seem to be more given to learning. They are inquisitive, and are full of ingenuity. Children ask a lot of questions. It should be noted that at the point when we stop asking questions, we stop learning. The old adage "you can't teach an old dog new tricks" has some merit. Jesus said, "You can't put new wine in old wineskins."

The good news is that new wineskins are possible by the renewing of your mind. There is a segment of the adult generation whose growth has been stunted relative to the information and technology era in which we live. They refuse to ask questions. And they are finding themselves unequipped to live a quality life with at least a working knowledge of the computer and Internet. Likewise, there is a generation of adults who in their own mind cannot be transformed to a childlike character relative to praise and worship. Sadly, they will find themselves living out the rest of their lives less than victorious, and beneath God's purpose and provisions.

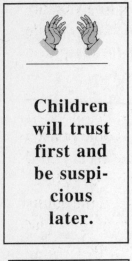

Children will trust first and be suspicious later.

It is important not to stifle our children, but to teach them and allow them to praise and worship God.

4. Children will trust first and be suspicious later. Actually, in some cases, this is a well-learned lesson. Trusting people has caused many to become suspicious and untrusting. However, we are in this case refusing to trust God. God has never hurt any one who trusted in Him and He never will. Children trust their parents based on a parent's promise. Oftentimes, promises are broken and likewise, trust is broken. But, God is a promise keeper! He promised if you trust him he will make your enemies your footstool. He promises there is victory in praise. He has provided praise as a weapon against evil. We must trust his provision.

Conclusions

1. It is important not to stifle our children, but to teach them and allow them to praise and worship God. One of my regrets is that while my children were young, I did not teach them how to praise and worship God. While they are young,

we should teach them how to praise and worship God. While they are young, we should teach them more than just their prayers at night and to bless their food before they eat. We should teach them how to praise and worship God even in the house in quiet time and devotions. If we do, they may not have the problems we adults have struggled with concerning praising God. An adult having to go back and be set free to be able to praise and worship God with a childlike behavior is not always easy. While they are young and coachable, teach children how to praise and worship God. After all, it's easy for them.

Praise is evangelistic.

2. <u>Praise is evangelistic.</u> In our opening scripture reference, the people praised and worshiped God collectively and loudly. It is not unreasonable to believe that the children saw and heard the adults give Jesus this public praise. The children's behavior in the temple was an exact duplication of the behavior exhibited by the people during Jesus' triumphant entrance into Jerusalem. Our behavior as adults **will and does** have an impact on our children.

Unfortunately, they learn both the good and the bad from us. We must share the good news of the gospel and exhibit our gratitude for the King of kings through our praise and worship of Him. God will perfect the praise that is already in them. As we follow the children's example of honest, uninhibited praise, we will surely end up *praising the hell right out of ourselves!*

Skull Practice
Chapter Eight -- Praising the Hell Out of Yourself
With a Childlike Character

1. Are children easily intimidated?

No! However, unlike children, adults are more likely to be intimidated by what others think and perceive them to be.

2. Who are more uninhibited, children or adults?

Children are much more uninhibited than adults. Adults have been trained through the developmental stages of life to simply be cautious in all their endeavors.

3. List four behaviors of children that make their praise more genuine before the Lord.

(a) children are not easily intimidated
(b) children are uninhibited in their actions
(c) children are teachable and coachable
(d) children will trust first and be suspicious later

4. Should we teach children to praise?

Yes! It is important that we do not stifle their praise. We should teach them how to praise His word through our example.

Fill in the blanks

1. In order for us to enter into the presence of the Lord and praise the hell out of ourselves we must adopt a _____ character. (childlike)

2.   Believers with a _____ character be- .
lieve that their heavenly father loves them so much that
He will move heaven and earth just to make sure that they
are all right. (childlike)

3.   _____ is what God desires
and rewards. (Childlikeness)

4.   _____ is a prerequisite for
entrance into the kingdom of heaven as well as a key to
enter into His presence in worship. (Childlikeness)

5.   We miss the opportunity to properly praise and
worship God because we put away _____
_____. _____ rather than _____.
(childlikeness) (childishness)

What will be the outcome of ignoring the teaching in this chapter?

1.   You will never know and experience the security of having a heavenly father.

2.   You run the risk of not being able to praise the hell out of
yourself because of intimidation.

3.   You run the risk of not being able to praise the hell out of
yourself due to adult developmental inhibitions.

4.   You run the rusk of putting your children in jeopardy of
never knowing the power of praise.

Helpful dialogue

1. Discuss the author's assertion that, "If you really want to know how to praise the hell out of yourself, become as dependent on God as a baby is dependent upon his parents."

2. Discuss some biblical examples of childlike behavior mentioned in this chapter that resulted in victory.

3. Discuss the meaning of Jesus' words when He said, "Out of the mouth of babes and sucklings thou hast perfected praise."

4. Discuss the relationship of adult behavior to children's praise.

Chapter 9
Praising the Hell Out of Yourself
With a Sacrifice

*And Araunah said unto David, Let my lord the king take
and offer up what seemeth good unto him: behold, here
be oxen for burnt sacrifice, and threshing instruments
and other instruments of the oxen for wood. ... And the
king said unto Araunah, Nay; but I will surely buy it of
thee at a price: neither will I offer burnt offerings unto
the Lord my God of that which doth cost me nothing.
So David bought the threshingfloor and the oxen
for fifty shekels of silver*
II Samuel 24:22, 24

*By him therefore let us offer the sacrifice of praise to
God continually, that is, the fruit of our lips giving
thanks to his name.*
Hebrews 13:15

*I beseech you therefore, brethren, by the mercies of God,
that ye present your bodies a living sacrifice, holy,
acceptable unto God, which is your reasonable service.*
Romans 12:1

As we begin this chapter on "Praising the Hell out of
Yourself with a Sacrifice," simply meditate upon King
David's profound statement (paraphrased), **I will not offer anything (including praise & worship) unto the Lord
which did not cost me anything.** What an awesome
thought! Because we live in a day and age when there are
so many demands upon us, somehow we have begun to
believe that everything we do is now a sacrifice. Spending

> **Sacrifice means "the forfeiture of something highly valued, as an idea, object, or friendship, for the sake of someone or something considered to have a greater value or claim."**

time with our children—a sacrifice. Spending time directing the choir is a sacrifice. Going to Bible Study and Sunday School is a sacrifice.

As difficult as it is to participate in these and other activities, we must seriously ask ourselves how many of those things are more of an inconvenience because of misplaced priorities we've placed on ourselves rather than genuine sacrifices. By definition, sacrifice means "the forfeiture of something highly valued, as an idea, object, or friendship, for the sake of someone or something considered to have a greater value or claim."[1] Each of us will place a different value upon the things we do, as well as the people in our lives. However, in order to come into God's presence with a sacrifice, we must realize that there is nothing greater than God—nothing.

Our primary emphasis in this chapter will be to better understand how sacrifice is more of a condition of the heart which will be seen in the things a person physically gives or offers to the Lord. Throughout the bible, both physical and spiritual sacrifice was required and exhibited when men and women desired the intimacy and presence of God. Note the following examples of sacrifice.

- *[3]And in the process of time it came to pass, that Cain brought of the fruit of the ground an offering unto the Lord. [4]And Abel, he also brought of the firstlings of his flock and of the fat thereof. And the Lord had respect unto Abel and to his offering: ⁵But unto Cain and to his offering he had not respect. And Cain was very wroth, and his countenance fell. Genesis 4:3-5.* Abel gave God the best from his firstlings. The bible simply says that his brother Cain brought of the fruit of the ground. It did not distinguish his offering as a "first fruits." Therefore, it was not a sacrifice.

- ⁹*And they came to the place which God had told him of; and Abraham built an altar there, and laid the wood in order, and bound Isaac his son, and laid him on the altar upon the wood. ¹⁰And Abraham stretched forth his hand, and took the knife to slay his son. ¹¹And the angel of the Lord called unto him out of heaven, and said, Abraham, Abraham: and he said, Here am I. ¹²And he said, Lay not thine hand upon the lad, neither do thou any thing unto him: for now I know that thou fearest God, seeing thou hast not withheld thy son,* **thine only son** *from me. (Bold added for emphasis).* Although Abraham had another son, Ishmael by his wife's handmaid, God did not recognize him. In fact, according to verse twelve (12) above, God referred to Isaac as Abraham's only son. Abraham was willing to sacrifice **his only** son because he placed a higher value on God and His request of him.

- ¹¹*And she vowed a vow, and said, O Lord of hosts, if thou wilt indeed look on the affliction of thine handmaid, and remember me, and not forget thine handmaid, but wilt give unto thine handmaid a man child, then I will give him unto the Lord all the days* *of his life, and there shall not razor come upon his head. ... [20]Wherefore it came to pass, when the time was come about after Hannah had conceived, that she bare a son, and called his name Samuel, saying, Because I have asked him of the Lord. ... [24]And when she had weaned him, she took him up with her, with three bullocks, and one ephah of flour, and a bottle of wine, and brought him unto the house of the Lord in Shiloh and the child was young. ... [27]For this child I prayed; and the Lord hath given me my petition which I asked of him: [28]Therefore also I have lent him to the Lord; as long as he liveth he shall be lent [granted] to the Lord. And he worshipped the Lord there. I Samuel 1:11, 20, 24, 27-28.* Hannah was loved by her husband but without a child that she desperately desired. As much as she wanted a child, she vowed to give him to the Lord **as a sacrifice**. She kept her promise to the Lord and turned the child over to Eli the priest **during a time of worship**.

- *[31]And, behold, thou shalt conceive in thy womb, and bring forth a son, and shalt call his name Jesus. ... [34]Then said Mary unto the angel, How shall this be, seeing I know not a man? [35]And the angel answered and said unto her, The Holy Ghost shall come upon thee, and the power of the Highest shall overshadow thee: therefore also that holy thing which shall be born of thee shall be called the Son of God. ... [38]And Mary said, Behold the handmaid of the Lord; be it unto me according to thy word. And the angel departed from her. Luke 1:31, 34-35, 38.* Mary was an unmarried woman who could be killed for having a child out of wedlock. Because of her love for God, she sacrificed her body, reputation, life and child because she placed more value on God than she did the things that concerned her.

- *¹⁸And Jesus, walking by the sea of Galilee, saw two brethren, Simon called Peter, and Andrew his brother, casting a net into the sea: for they were fishers. ¹⁹And he saith unto them, Follow me, and I will make you fishers of men. ²⁰And they straightway left their nets, and followed him. Matthew 4:18-20. ²⁸Then Peter began to say unto him, Lo, **we have left all**, and have followed thee. Luke 10:28 (Bold added for emphasis).* Peter and Andrew were successful fishermen. Along with their business partners, James & John (Luke 5:10), they left their fishing businesses to follow One greater and of more value.

- *¹⁴I am the good shepherd, and know my sheep, and am known of mine. ¹⁵As the Father knoweth me, even so know I the Father: and I lay down my life for the sheep. ¹⁶And other sheep I have, which are not of this fold: them also I must bring, and they shall hear my voice; and there shall be one fold, and one shepherd. ¹⁷Therefore doth my Father love me, because I lay down my life, that I might take it again. ¹⁸**No man taketh it from me, but I lay it down of myself.** I have power to lay it down, and I have power to take it again. This commandment have I received of my Father. John 10:14-18 (Bold added for emphasis.)* God the Son valued the commandment of God the Father so much that He **voluntarily** sacrificed Himself for His sheep.

Sacrifice is as much a condition of the heart as it is the resulting action. In each of the previous instances, sacrifice was given to God out of a deep reverence and recognition of His worth and value. The things each willingly gave is a testimony of the love, faith, and awe each had in his heart for God and His Word. What about you? How much are you in need of the presence of God? How much are you willing to sacrifice so that the hell in your life can be eradicated? Before we attempt to answer those questions, let's look at how a sacrifice is often made to God.

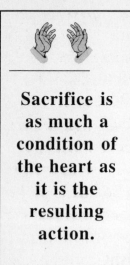

Sacrifice is as much a condition of the heart as it is the resulting action.

From Genesis through the New Testament, there was often some form of an altar built to offer God the physical sacrifice. In the Old Testament, the altar was often a physical structure while in the New Testament, the altar was more often made of the faith in a person's heart. Because sacrifice is a prerequisite to worship, a close observation must be made as to what we are sacrificing as Living Testaments. It can often translate into the difference between victory or defeat, life or death, and continued bondage or salvation. Take the following event for example.

In baseball, there is a play called the sacrifice. During a game between the Atlanta Braves and Florida, the Braves could not sacrifice the runner in the scoring position, so they lost the game. The sacrifice play is described as follows. If the runner is at one base and you want to move him ahead, the batter gives up his opportunity to hit a homerun. He gives up his opportunity to make a hit. The batter gives up his opportunity to get on first base and improve his batting average.

He simply bunts the ball, knowing that he is going to get out and his average will decrease rather than increase. With all that in mind, the batter sacrifices all individual benefits of a homerun because he places more value on the potential for the team. In other words, the essence of sacrifice is giving up something **that you real - l - l - l -y want, value, deserve, cherish and brings you benefit.** There is no such thing as a sacrifice without giving up something.

In the book of Malachi, God teaches us something about sacrifice as it relates to tithing. Worship had become vain. The people were not giving God the best of what they had. The scripture paints the picture of them choosing any old lamb, the runt of the litter, the one which might die tomorrow anyway, as a offering to God.

Can you see it. The little lamb's hair is all matted to his body. The lamb was so scroungy looking that the whole family would prefer peanut butter and jelly sandwiches for dinner instead of a rack of lamb! Yet, this was the type of offering the people were making and they had the nerve to think it was a sacrifice!

[7]*Ye offer polluted bread upon mine altar; and ye say, Wherein have we polluted thee? In that ye say, The table of the Lord is contemptible.* [8]*And if ye offer the blind for sacrifice, is it not evil? and if ye offer the lame and sick, it is not evil? offer it now unto thy governor; will he be pleased with thee, or accept thy person? saith the Lord of hosts. ...* [10]*Who is there even among you that would shut the doors for nought? neither do ye kindle fire on mine altar for nought [in vain]. I have no pleasure in you, saith the Lord of hosts, neither will I accept an offering at your hand. ...* [13]*Ye said also, Behold, what a weariness is it!*

and ye have snuffed at it, saith the Lord of hosts; and ye
brought that which was torn [taken by violence], and the
lame, and the sick; thus ye brought an offering; should
I accept this of your hand? saith the Lord. [14]But cursed
be the deceiver, which hath in his flock a male, and voweth,
and sacrificed unto the Lord a corrupt [blemished]
thing: for I am a great King, saith the Lord of
hosts, and my name is dreadful among the heathen.
Malachi 1:7-8, 10, 13-14

God described their sacrifice as lame and sick and accused them of snuffing (turning up their noses) at His altar. Today, many believers bring a lame praise and snuff at

Even though God daily provides us with new mercies, we often give Him our leftovers hoping that He will accept them.

the thought of entering into His presence in expressive, active worship. Even though God daily provides us with new mercies, we often give Him our leftovers hoping that He will accept them.

After all, you could have paid two car payments rather than giving Him your tithe. You could have made some overtime to get that new furniture instead of going to Bible Study. Certainly He would be pleased that you agreed to teach a Discipleship Class at church when you could be teaching at the local Seminary! Pleased? I think not.

When we offer God the sacrifice of praise, we give Him praise rather than placing more value on *"not feeling good"* or *"not getting sweaty in our new suit,"* or *"not looking fanatical in front of that person you're trying to impress"* or *"maintaining our prideful, holier than thou*

> **Our lack of sacrifice not only affect the things we withhold from God. It is also displayed in our attitude toward those things.**

look." Therefore, our lack of sacrifice not only affect the things we withhold from God. It is also displayed in our attitude toward those things.

In II Samuel 24:18, King David paid a severe penalty for his attitude of pride. The prophet of God told the king to go and number the people. David taking the lead from the man of God went and counted the people. Upon doing so, David succumbed to the temptation of pride. In numbering the people, he began to feel too good about himself and/or accomplishments.

How often in our churches to do we talk about numbers and how much our membership and budgets have grown. There is a warning here. Although God instructed David to number the people, he punished the people for taking pride in those numbers.

God sent punishment on David and he realized the sin of pride. God gave him three choices for his punishment: 1) pestilence, 2) war, or 3) famine. Instead of choosing the one he was obvious good at (David was known as a successful man of war), he chose pestilence because he felt that he would rather trust God's mercy rather than his ability. Not only did his choice show his repentant spirit, it also showed his confidence in the mercies of God. As the scripture continues, we see that many people died as a result of the pestilence sent by God. However, in the midst of the pestilence, David is instructed to go and worship God. When he could have been bitter, pouting or trying to hold onto *"the numbers,"* David chose to **sacrificially obey** and go worship God.   David chose to sacrificially praise the punishment he deserved out of his life.

After arriving at the threshing place of Araunah the Jebusite, everything for the sacrifice was already there for David. There were oxen, threshing instruments and other instruments, which Araunah offered to **give** to David so that he could offer a sacrifice to the Lord.

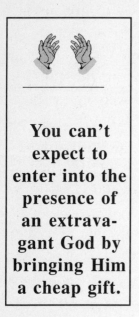

You can't expect to enter into the presence of an extravagant God by bringing Him a cheap gift.

However, David refused to accept the items for free and paid Araunah fifty shekels of silver for the items. Fifty shekels of silver was a small price to pay after David had already sacrificed his will to obey God! Additionally, David recognized that you can't expect to enter into the presence of an extravagant God by bringing Him a cheap gift.

Unfortunately, today we often fall short of bringing God the sacrifice He desires. Some of us buy new homes and have them dedicated. Periodically, we engage in Parent/Child dedication of our children. God blesses us with a new car and we commit to picking up as many people as possible for church. We discover our spiritual gifts and resolve to use them in the church in one of the various ministry opportunities. However, as good and necessary as all of those commitments are, they all fall short of the sacrifice that God desires most which will quickly usher you behind the veil and into the presence of God.

[1]I beseech you therefore, brethren, by the mercies of God,
that ye present your bodies a living sacrifice, holy,
acceptable unto God, which is your
reasonable service.   Romans 12:1

The sacrifice God desires more than anything is something we often value more than Him. We are the sacrifice that God wants. God doesn't just want our gifts, talents and other resources. He wants us to totally surrender our total being to His Lordship. He knows that if we would do that, all those other things would easily follow.

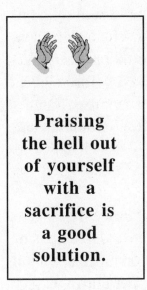

Praising the hell out of yourself with a sacrifice is a good solution.

Many people need to be delivered from the spirit of idolatry because we value ourselves more than God. However, praising the hell out of yourself with a sacrifice is a good solution. We refuse to surrender every aspect of who we are over to Christ. Rather than placing our total being on the altar, we hold onto things that we're not ready to render over to holiness and acceptability to God. Yet, God, through the Apostle Paul, tells us that **totally** giving ourselves is **the sacrifice** and our reasonable act of worship.   In other words, if we reason with ourselves on who God is and what God has done, we will give Him a sacrifice of praise.

Conclusion

1. There are two times to praise and worship God. When you feel like it and when you don't feel like it. When you don't feel like it, that's a type of sacrifice. Remember, in

the midst of the pestilence, David offered God the sacrifice of praise. The writer of Hebrews tells us that "By him therefore, let us offer the sacrifice of praise to God continually, that is, the fruit of our lips, giving thanks to his name" (Hebrews 13:15). If you have a loss in your family, you probably will not feel like praising God. Yet you should still praise Him.

When we have losses and our hearts are breaking, we should still praise Him. If your children are rebelling, your spouse leaving, your body aching or your job cutting back, you should still offer God the sacrifice of praise. Your feelings or situations should not be placed before or dictate the worthiness of His worship. Also remember, Satan's most opportune time to enter into your life is when you are not feeling good. Praise will keep him at a distance as well as chase him out.

2.   Giving God sacrificial praise will cost you to give something that you hold in high value to the One who is of the highest value. You will never be a worshiper until you are a giver. You will never be a worshipper until you recognize that God is supreme and nothing we have or can do is commensurate to His worth. Our total giving of ourselves is the ultimate testimony of God's headship. While all the world seeks to heap riches, glory, and honor upon themselves, the people of God should continually give themselves, and their possessions, attitudes, and emotions over to the One who created us. God always has our best interest at heart.

3.   Salvation, the ultimate sacrifice, cost Jesus His life. We often hear people say that salvation is free. However, the atoning act on the cross of Calvary cost Jesus Christ

His life! No other sacrifice has or will cost more. Jesus' primary desire was to please the Father by doing His will. The bible clearly tells us that it pleased the Father for Jesus to suffer the agony of the cross (Isaiah 53:10). Jesus' entire sinless life, willing death, necessary burial and triumphant resurrection all bought praise and glory to the Father. In the same manner, fulfillment of the process of discipleship will also bring praise and glory to God.

Discipleship will cost the "would-be" disciple something. Just like Jesus, one must sacrificially surrender their total will. Although you probably will not have to travel up Golgatha's Hill, you will have to take up your own cross daily and follow Christ's example. The bible says that the disciples sacrificed all to follow Christ. Because of their obedience, the Christian church was born to the glory and praise of God!

4. Discipleship Costs. Salvation is free but discipleship costs. Discipleship may cost but the price is right. The price is the cost of presenting our bodies as a living sacrifice, holy, acceptable unto God, which is our reasonable (worship) service.

Endnote:

[1]Morris, William, Editor, *The American Heritage Dictionary of the English Language* (New York, NY: American Heritage)

Skull Practice
Chapter Nine — Praising the Hell Out of Yourself
With a Sacrifice

1. What is a sacrifice?

A sacrifice is the forfeiture of something highly valued, such as an idea, object, or friendship, for the sake of someone or something considered to have a greater value or claim.

2. What does a sacrifice of praise mean?

This simply means that we should give God our praise regardless of our circumstances and situations.

3. What is the ultimate sacrifice God wants from us?

Ultimately, God wants us. The Bible says that this is our reasonable service (Romans 12:1). He wants us to totally surrender our being to His Lordship.

4. How are we to give God a sacrifice that is pleasing to Him?

Present our bodies as a living sacrifice, holy, acceptable unto God, which is our reasonable service (worship).

Fill in the blanks

1. _____ is as much a condition of the heart as is the resulting action. (Sacrifice)

2. To come into God's presence with a _____, we must recognize that there is nothing greater than God. (sacrifice)

3. _____ is a prerequisite to worship. (Sacrifice)

4. To _____ means giving up something you really want, value, desire, cherish, and brings you benefit. (Sacrifice)

5. There is no such thing as a _____ without giving up something. (sacrifice)

What will be the outcome of ignoring the teaching in this chapter?

1. You will never be a complete worshiper.

2. You will never be available to be fully used by God.

3. You will run the risk of being bound up by an evil spirit.

4. You run the risk of never having a clean heart and a renewed spirit.

5. You will never be a team player.

Helpful dialogue

1.   Discuss some biblical examples of sacrifice referenced in this chapter.

2.   Discuss the difference between an inconvenience and a sacrifice.

3.   Discuss how much you are willing to sacrifice so that the hell in your life can be eradicated.

4.   Elaborate on David's biblical statement, "Neither will I offer burnt offerings unto the Lord my God of that which doth cost me nothing. (2 Samuel 24:22,24). What are the implications to our contemporary Christian journey?

5.   Elaborate on the statement that, "Salvation is free but discipleship costs."

Chapter 10
Praising the Hell out of Yourself Through the Use of His Names

For we rest on thee and in thy name we go against
this multitude.
Lord, thou art our God; let not man prevail against thee.
II Chronicles 14:11b

If ye shall ask any thing in my name, I will do it.
John 14:14

I have many memories of my childhood years. For example, I can remember when we used to get all dress up on Saturday afternoon with expectations of having a "good time" Saturday evening. I specifically remember taking my Saturday bath early and preparing my hair with some Vaseline to give it some shine. If I had some, I'd put on a little cheap toilet water cologne and get ready to go stand on the block or maybe even go to the movie. Just as I was getting ready to leave, a voice would call out and say something like, "Remember, your name is McCalep."

After those words were uttered, all plans for getting into some questionable activities simply vanished. I knew that no matter what I desired to do, those words would follow me throughout the evening and quite possibly "rain on my parade." Many of our parents and grandparents may not have had a lot of education. What they did have was good solid morals and dignity. This was the message they tried to convey to us as we exited the confines of home where all of our "home training" needed to be displayed.

There is something in a name.

In those days, and still today, there is a notion that there is something in a name. I can remember being asked on a number of occasions, "Who are your people?" Value was placed on maintaining the dignity of the family name and our parents wanted to make sure the activities of Saturday evening didn't destroyed something that took several generations to build.

So it is at an even higher level with the name(s) of God. Mighty is the name of God (Jer. 10:6). It is in God's

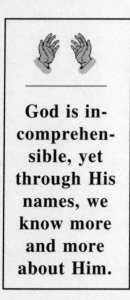

God is incomprehensible, yet through His names, we know more and more about Him.

name that we find out the real person He is. It is in His name that we discover His manifold nature and character. God's names provide us with a self-revelation of who our Heavenly Father is. Although we use human language to identify Him, His names and character is uniquely divine. Interestingly enough, God is incomprehensible, yet through His names, we know more and more about Him. Two suggestions can be made regarding God's names:

·   God wants us to know Him through His names to the degree He is willing to reveal Himself to us.
·   God wants us to know Him through His names to the degree we are willing to experience Him.

Because God is infinite, finite man will never be able to fully comprehend all there is about our Father. Even as we sit and think about all of who He is, many times we end

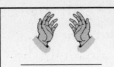

God has promised us that we can invoke His power by calling on His name.

up defining Him based on what He is or has done. We may begin praising by simply calling His name, but if we stay in an attitude of praise for any period of time, we will begin to think about all He's done for us and begin to praise Him for His mighty acts of mercy. God has promised us that we can invoke His power by calling on His name. Consider the following scriptures.

And whatsoever ye shall ask in my name, that will I do, that the Father may be glorified in the Son.   John 14:13

But these are written, that ye might believe that Jesus is the Christ, the Son of God; and that believing ye might have life through his name.
John 21:31

Then Peter said, Silver and gold have I none; but such as I have give I thee In the name of Jesus Christ of Nazareth rise up and walk.
Acts 3:6

Be it known unto you all, and to all the people of Israel, that by the name of Jesus Christ of Nazareth, whom ye crucified, whom God raised from the dead, even by him doth this man stand here before you whole.
Acts 4:10

And this did she many days, But Paul, being grieved, turned and said to the spirit, I command thee in the name of Jesus Christ to come out of her. And he came out the same hour.
Acts 16:18

*Giving thanks always for all things unto God and the Father
in the name of our Lord Jesus Christ.*
Ephesians 5:20

If you call Him Jehovah-Jireh—which means God our provider—and you think about how you experienced his provisions when you could not help yourself, you may find yourself praising him shamelessly. If you call Him Jehovah Rophi—which means God our Healer—and you think about how he healed your body, the praise you have on the inside may break out on the outside.

His name is to be praised. His name is so powerful that we can praise the hell out of ourselves in His name.

The scriptures indicate that there is strength in His name. Evil can be cast out in His name. Salvation comes through His name. There is healing in His name. Thanksgiving should be given in His name. His name is to be praised. His name is so powerful that we can praise the hell out of ourselves in His name.

A Biblical Illustration of Victory in His Name – II Chronicles 14:11

Chronicled in the Old Testament is one of many historical narratives where the enemy was defeated and victory was gained through the use of His name. Asa—who was the son of Abijah, the grandson of Rehoboam and the great grandson of Solomon—was now King. Asa was a good king and found favor with God. He is known to have started the first revival in the Southern Kingdom There were no revivals, neither were there any good kings (not a single one) from the Northern Kingdom. Asa tore down the altars of all the idol gods—Asa was a man of peace. However, the Ethiopian army made war against him. Asa called on the name of the Lord and gained the victory.

*And Asa cried unto the Lord his God, and said, Lord it is
nothing with thee to Help, whether with many, or with
them that have no power: help us, O Lord Our God; for we
rest on thee, and in thy name we go against this multitude.
O Lord, thou art our God; let not man prevail against thee.
So the Lord Some the Ethiopians before Asa, and before
Judah; and the Ethiopians fled.*
II Chronicles 14:11-12

God's name is powerful in praise and prayer. There-fore, all our prayers and praise ought to be done in His name. However, when we come before His presence we ought to be coming in His name. So we lift up holy hands in His name; we sing in His name; we shout in His name; we praise Him with the dance in His name. We praise the hell out of ourselves in His name. For indeed His name is worthy to be praised.

*Praise ye the Lord. Praise,
O ye servants of the Lord,
praise the name of the Lord.
Blessed be the name of the Lord
from this time forth and for evermore.
From the Rising of the sun
unto the going down of the same
the Lord's name is to be praised.*
Psalm 113:1-3

Included in this chapter is a brief list of some names of God, their meanings and scripture references. Many times

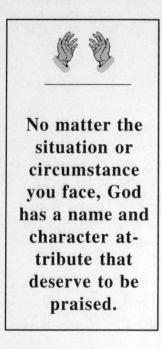

No matter the situation or circumstance you face, God has a name and character attribute that deserve to be praised.

in scripture, God revealed Himself and the person experienced God in a special way which caused them to use various forms of His name. No matter the situation or circumstance you face, God has a name and character attribute that deserve to be praised.

One name for God is **Elohim**. **Elohim** means Creator.

Through faith we understand that the worlds were framed by the word of God, so that things which are seen were not made of things which do appear. **Hebrews 11:3**

This name of God was one of the first used for Him in scripture. In the book of Genesis, we see **Elohim** creating the universe and mankind. To understand the awesomeness of the name **Elohim**, we must understand the difference between a "creator" and a "maker". A creator takes nothing and makes something. A "maker" takes something that already exists and makes something else from it. The name **Elohim** is unique only to our Father because He is the ONLY ONE who has taken nothing and made something out of it.

At the darkest point in our lives, **Elohim** stepped into our darkness and said, "Let there be light at the end of the tunnel. Or as in the case of Abraham and Sarah, "Let there be a baby to come forth from a 100 year old man and a 90 year old woman!" God took the nothingness of Sarah's womb and made her husband the Father of many nations.

When you think about that, you can't help but praise the name of **Elohim**!

Then there's the name **El Shaddai** which means The All Sufficient One.

> *And lest I should be exalted above measure through the abundance of the revelations, there was given to me a thorn in the flesh, the messenger of Satan to buffet me, lest I should be exalted above measure. For this thing I besought the Lord thrice, that it might depart from me. And he said unto me, My grace is sufficient for thee: for my strength is made perfect in weakness. Most gladly therefore will I rather glory in my infirmities, that the power of Christ may rest upon me. Therefore I take pleasure in infirmities, in reproaches, in necessities, in persecutions, in distresses for Christ's sake: for when I am weak, then am I strong. II Corinthians 12:7-10*

Many times in our lives, we spend far too much time trying to obtain more because we don't feel we have enough or trying to get rid of something we don't want or like. We move from relationship to relationship in hopes of finding Mr. or Ms. Right. Unfortunately, those individuals seem to fall short of our expectations and we move on becoming more and more disappointed with each new relationship. Often the problem is not the other person.

The problem is sometimes the expectation we place upon them to fulfill a need that can only be filled through a relationship with **El Shaddai**. Wrapped in God's name, **El Shaddai,** is the sum total of everything we will ever need. If we need more love, **El Shaddai**. If you need more understanding, **El Shaddai**. If we need more grace, **El Shaddai**. Whatever the need, **El Shaddai** is well able to supply it. The name **El Shaddai** also conveys the message that God will keep His promises as He did with

Abraham. Think of your greatest need and begin praising
El Shaddai.

Another one of God's names is **Adonai** which means
The Lord. Notice this name for God means <u>The</u> Lord, not
just "a lord" or lord.

> *Behold, as the eyes of servants look unto the hand of their*
> *masters, and as the eyes of a maiden unto the hand of her*
> *mistress; so our eyes wait upon the* LORD *our God, until that*
> *he have mercy upon us.   Psalm 123:2*

There are many things which will seek to "lord" over
us -- No matter the situation or circumstance you face, God
has a name and character attribute that deserve to be praised
-- our emotions, careers, spouses, creditors, and even well
meaning family members. But there is only one true **Lord**
and He wants to have complete headship in our lives. When
The Lord is in control, much of the stress and pressures
we place upon ourselves will be removed. **The Lord,** who
is also **El Shaddai**, is well able to take care of us. In fact,
if nothing already exists to secure His promise to us, simply remember His name is also **Elohim**. He can take nothing and make something and then work it for your good!
Praise the name of **Adonai**!

One of the most popular names for God is **Jehovah.**
Jehovah means The Self-Existent One. In other words,
God has always been God and no one played a part in His
beginning. He is who He is because of who He was, is and
will be. That thought is so awesome, it bears repeating.
Jehovah is who He is because of who He was, is and will
be.

> *And Moses said unto God, Behold, when I come unto the*
> *children of Israel, and shall say unto them, The God of your*
> *fathers hath sent me unto you; and they shall say to me, What*

is his name? what shall I say unto them? And God said unto Moses, I AM THAT I AM: and he said, Thus shalt thou say unto the children of Israel, I AM hath sent me unto you.
Exodus 3:13-14

When Moses met God on Mt. Horeb, **Jehovah** presented Moses a mission opportunity. After explaining to him what he was to do, Moses asked God what His name was. Notice, Moses did not name God. **Jehovah** named Himself. He said, **"I Am That I Am."** I am everything good and perfect. Everything that I am is because of who I am.

The name **Jehovah** is so great and full that addendums were added to it as man experienced Him is new ways. For example, many of us have experienced God as **Jehovah Jireh**, The Lord My Provider. When we came up "short" and our back was against the wall, **Jehovah Jireh** has shown up and provided everything we needed. Look at what He did for Abraham.

And the angel of the LORD called unto him out of heaven, and said, Abraham, Abraham: and he said, Here am I. And he said, Lay not thine hand upon the lad, neither do thou any thing unto him: for now I know that thou fearest God, seeing thou hast not withheld thy son, thine only son from me. And Abraham lifted up his eyes, and looked, and behold behind him a ram caught in a thicket by his horns: and Abraham went and took the ram, and offered him up for a burnt offering in the stead of his son. And Abraham called the name of that place Jehovah-jireh: as it is said to this day, In the mount of the LORD it shall be seen.
Genesis 22:11-14

Note the significant superlative relative to His name. First, all that God is, He is in His name. Second, all that He is in His name, he is in Christ. Christ is in all the names. And third, all that He is in Christ He is in us. Read carefully these words of God and prepare for praise to rise up in you.

> *That they all may be one; as thou, Father, art in me, and I*
> *in thee, that they also may be on in us: that the world*
> *may believe that thou hast sent me...And I have declared*
> *unto them thy **name**, and will declare it: that the love*
> *wherewith thou hast loved me may be in them,*
> *and I in them.*
> *John 17:21, 26*

When people hear your name, what do they think about? What kind of legacy has attached itself to your name? All of us have relatives who have made mistakes. Or maybe you were the one that made the mistake and cost your "family name" some shame. Don't be discouraged. The Bible tells us that we have a new identifier. A new family with a new Daddy and a new name. As you read the names of God mentioned in this chapter and their meaning, please recognize that this is not an exhaustive list. It will, however, provide you with a good foundation for praying and *praising the hell right out of yourself* by using the names of God.

NAME	MEANING	SCRIPTURE LOCATION
Elohim	Creator	Gen 1:2-3, Heb 11:3; Gen 1:26
El Elyon	God Most High	Dan 4:34, 35
El Roi	God Who Sees	Psa 121:1-4; II Thes 1:5-10
El Olam	The Everlasting God	Gen 21:33
El Shaddai	The All Sufficient One	Gen 17:1-8; II Cor 12:9-10
Adonai	The Lord	Phil 1:20-21; Luke 6:46; Psa 123:2
Jehovah	The Self-Existent One	Ex 3:1-15
Jehovah-Jireh	The Lord My Provider	Gen 22:1-19; Phil 4:19
Jehovah Rophe	The Lord My Healer	II Kin 20:1, 4-5; II Chr 7:14; Isa 19:22, 53:5; Ex 15:26
Jehovah Nissi	The Lord My Banner	Ex 17:15-16; Num 21:1-8; John 3:14-15
Jehovah M'Kaddesh	The Lord My Sanctifier	Ex 19:2-6; I Pet 2:9; Ex 10:10-14 31:12-18; Heb 10:10-14; Lev 20:8
Jehovah Shalom	The Lord My Peace	I Thes 5:23; Num 6:22-27; Isa 26:3; Phil 4:4-9; Jud 6:24
Jehovah Saboath (tsebaah)	The Lord of Hosts	I Sam 1:1-3; 6-7, 10-11, 17:42-47; Psalm 46:7
Jehovah Rohi	The Lord My Shepherd	Psalm 23; John 10:1-10
Jehovah Tsidkenu	The Lord Our Righteousness	Jer 23:1-6; Eze 36:26-27; Mat 1:23; II Cor 5:21
Jehovah Shammah	The Lord Who is Present with me	Col 3:1-2; Psa 73:25-28; Eze 48:35
Ancient of Days	Before the Beginning; The Judge	Dan 7:9-22

Skull Practice
Chapter Ten - Praising the Hell Out of Yourself
Through the Use of His Names

1. Can we learn about God through His names?
Yes, we can learn about God through His names. God reveals Himself through His names.

2. What does the name Jehoval Jireh mean?
It means God our provider.

3. What does the name Jehovah Rapha mean?
It mans God our healer.

4.   When can we call on the name of Jesus?
Anytime and at all times; and in the time of trouble.

5. When should we always call on the name of Jesus?
Always in praise and prayer.

6.   List three superlaties relative to His name.
(a) All that God is, He is in His name
(b) All that He is in His name, He is in Christ
(c) All that He is in Christ, He is in us

Fill in the blanks

1. There is something in a _____. (name)

2.   It is in God's _____ that we find out the real person He is. (name)

3. Mighty is the _____ of God. (name)

4. God has promised us that we can invoike His power by calling on His _____. (name)

5. Evil can be cast out in His _____. (name)

6. His _____ is so powerful that we can praise the hell out of ourselves in His _____. (name) (name)

What will be the outcome of ignoring the teaching in this chapter?

1. You will miss knowing and experiencing the fullness of who God really is.

2. You will experience His presence in your individual specific circumstances and situations.

3. The power of prayer will be weakened in your personal prayer life.

4. Your praise will be diluted, making you more vulnerable to the enemy.

Helpful dialogue

1. Discuss the biblical promises God gies to us through His name.

2. Discuss the various names of God in relationship to what they personally mean to you.

3. Discuss the biblical illustration mentioned in this chapter where the enemy of God's people were defeated and victory was gained through the use of His name.

4. Discuss the implications of the superlative list in this chapter relative to His names.

Chapter 11
Praising the Hell Out of Yourself With the Highest Praise - Hallelujah

And it came to pass in the fifth year of king Rehoboam, that Shishak king if Egypt came up against Jerusalem: And he took away the treasures of the house of the LORD, and the treasures of the king's house; he even took away all: and he took away all the shields of gold which Solomon had made. And king Rehoboam made in their stead brazen shields, and committed them unto the hands of the chief of the guard, which kept the door of the king's house.   I Kings 14:25-27

And after these things I heard a great voice of much people in heaven, saying, Alleluia; Salvation, and glory, and honour, and power, unto the Lord our God: For true and righteous are his judgments: for he hath judged the great whore, which did corrupt the earth with her fornication, and hath avenged the blood of his servants at her hand. And again they said, Alleluia. And her smoke rose up for ever and ever. And the four and twenty elders and the four beasts fell down and worshipped God that sat on the throne, saying, Amen; Alleluia. And a voice came out of the throne, saying, Praise our God, all ye his servants, and ye that fear him, both small and great. And I heard as it were the voice of a great multitude, and as the voice of mighty thunderings, saying, Alleluia: for the Lord God omnipotent reigneth.
Rev 19:1-6

Whether you know it or not, you may have been victimized by one of the cleverest robbers of all time. He's bold yet quite subtle. God has blessed me to preach and teach in rural churches as well as urban churches; large

Satan has entered far too many of our churches and has stolen one of the most precious jewels God has given us.

In the eyes of God, praise is priceless and possession and exercise of it can afford you the most valued privilege of all time — the presence of God!

churches as well as small churches; and to black congregations as well as white. In many of these churches, it became quite evident that the same robber had visited each. He left conclusive evidence of his visit by leaving his signature calling card; **the absence of praise**!

This robber, Satan, has entered far too many of our churches and has stolen one of the most precious jewels God has given us. This chapter will focus on the pricelessness of praise and our need to reclaim what has been stolen from many of us. The security locks on the doors of the church have been broken and the enemy has come in and stolen our precious, powerful strong gift of praise. We must take back and put back and put back the praise in our individual lives as well as in our congregations.

Why is stealing praise too important to Satan? There are a number of reasons. Foremost as indicated from the theme of this book it is a weapon given to the saints to be used against Satan in spiritual warfare. **When likened**

to the precious metal gold, praise is expensive and never loses value. In the eyes of God, praise is priceless and possession and exercise of it can afford you the most valued privilege of all time — the presence of God! Let me try to explain further.

I would venture to say that everyone has been introduced to or studied the properties of gold at some point in their life. Many of us who try to get by cheap when giving birthday and anniversary gifts have all too often had our "thriftiness" exposed. After being worn for even a short period of time, it becomes apparent to the gift receiver that the piece of jewelry was probably not purchased at a fine jewelry store.

In fact, based on the bumps and green ring around the affected area, chances are good that the once sparkling items was simply a cheap imitation of the real thing! Nothing beats the real thing. Authentic praise is costly. Among other things, it will cost you humbling yourself. It will cost you loving your neighbor as yourself. It will cost you to forgive those who hurt you. Unlike us, God will not accept anything other than the real thing! He doesn't have to try it on to see if it will change colors. He knows from the moment it was presented whether or not it is genuine.

Note the following interesting facts about gold.

1. In most societies, gold does not lose its value. Because it is considered the best, it can be used to obtain the best.

2. It has no inner impurities and will not tarnish. All that is required to restore any loss of brilliance is a simple polishing cloth.

3. When it is heated to a boiling point, it actually gets finer and more valuable.

4.   It can appear in many different forms (coins, jewelry, solid blocks, etc.), various intensities and grades (10K, 14K, 18K), and different colors (white or yellow).

5.   Its brilliance is most evident when the sun shines on the metal.

6.   Because of its beauty, its possession is envied by many. Because of its cost, it is often imitated.

Notice now these comparison as we compare praise to gold.

1.   The value of our praise and adoration to God will never depreciate. As we discussed in previous chapters, God desires and demands that we praise Him! Our Father enjoys for His creation to brag on Him. There is no greater sacrifice we can offer the Lord than a life yielding to the Lordship of Christ and a heart overflowing with praise. Nothing else is greater and holds more value.

2.   Genuine praise is pure praise. Just like gold, pure praise holds no inner impurities. When we offer God this costly praise, there are no hidden agendas. There is no evidence of hatred or malice toward your brother or sister. There is no secret sin hiding in the closet. There is no gossiping, back-biting or tale-bearing lurking by to tarnish your praise.

In fact, when pure praise is offered, you ultimately *praise the hell right out of yourself* and you are allowed to stand in the presence of a pure and Holy God. Often; however, our praise becomes dull and routine. All that is needed is the polishing cloth of prayer. As we pray and repent from engaging in praise and a religious activity, God polishes us off and our praise again become authentic.

3.   As the Spirit of God "turns up the heat" during praise, the praise being offered to God becomes more pronounced,

directed and intense. In a very true sense, your praise is being perfected by the refining fire of God. In the Refiner's fire, all of the impurities are burned away. All of the concerns you may have had when you began are no longer pressing upon you. The more intense the fire, the more you desire it. For you began to understand that the purer the praise, more of the presence of Jehovah God you experience. Praise God!

4. Praise is an individual thing. It doesn't matter whether your praise of gold appears as a fiery holy dance, a silent shedding of tears and raising of hands, the thunderous shout of "Hallelujah," or the humble bowing of the knee. God will receive them all. Because all of His children are uniquely different, the praise we offer to Him is exhibited differently with various degrees of intensity. I'm so glad, however, that He receives them all just the same.

5. During praise, there is no more awesome to witness than the glory of the Lord resting upon a person. Often during times of intense praise, the presence of the King will appear to consume a person. Many times, these individuals literally "pass out" under the power of the Holy Spirit. It is not uncommon to witness the brilliance of God's presence upon those individuals by the amazing, yet unexplainable appearance of their countenance.

6. Because of the beauty and liberality found in praise, it is often imitated and thus perverted. This can be seen more often in offering praise through dance and singing or music. Have you ever witnessed the following scene. You are in a church, or at a Christian concert and the music is playing. They are in perfect upbeat rhythm. The drums are racing. Then all of a sudden someone begins to shout

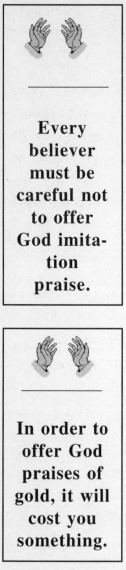

Every believer must be careful not to offer God imitation praise.

In order to offer God praises of gold, it will cost you something.

or dance. I mean, they really get into it. Then the music stops. What amazes me so much is that the shouting also stops in almost perfect timing! Now I'm not saying that that individual was not offering pure praise. However, it just appears odd that pure praise can be controlled like synchronized swimming.

Every believer must be careful not to offer God imitation praise. Imitation is sometimes mistaken for sacrificial praise. There are many times when you do not *"feel like"* praising God due to circumstances and various issues. In those times, we must press our way through to the throne of God recognizing that our help, hope and deliverance is all found in His presence. We must kick our *"feelings"* to the curb. Then there are times when people fake the shout; fake the singing, and unfortunately fake the tears. At these times, the forms of praise and worship are not genuine and are not pleasing to God. They can be classified as false praise and worship. Look what the Lord says about such types of praise and worship.

Ye worship ye know not what: we know what we worship: for salvation is of the Jews. [23]But the hour cometh, and now is, when the true worshippers shall worship the Father in spirit and in truth:

comparison to praise and gold, recognize that praise is the welcome mat for God is His own house. In other words, when we don't offer God genuine praise, we effectively remove any appearance of ushering and welcoming God into what belongs to Him anyway!

As tragic as this robber of the house of God was, it was not the most profound part of this misfortune. In my estimation, the most profound part of the estimation was that Rehoboam was not upset enough even to try and retrieve what had been stolen. In fact, he accepted this robbery and had the audacity to replace the shields with ones made of brass! He was willing and did settle for a cheap imitation. God was not esteemed high enough! I want to suggest to you that when anything else keeps us from offering God pure, costly praise, King Shishak has shown up again and stolen what rightfully belongs to God!

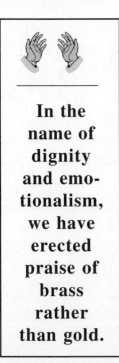

In the name of dignity and emotionalism, we have erected praise of brass rather than gold.

For example, in the name of dignity and emotionalism, we have erected praise of brass rather than gold. When we try to be so cute and dignified, we no longer shine like pure gold. We appear to be simply brass that looks good for the moment but **constantly** has to be polished. In like manner, when we become purely emotional in praise, we are like brass. Although we are emotional people, emotion is not praise. Praise is not based on how we feel or what makes us feel good. Praise is based wholly on the worthiness of God. Because King Solomon and his father, King David, understood the worthiness of

God, they would not compromise of giving Him what He alone desired. I can't image either one of them allowing any of God's gold to be replaced with brass. What about you? Even in the worst of situations, do you believe God is still worthy enough to offer Him praises of gold or will you compromise?

Gold Vs Hallelujah

Hallelujah holds the honor of denoting the highest praise. Like gold, hallelujah has universal value. Hallelujah has no language or cultural boundaries.

Hallelujah holds the honor of denoting the highest praise. Like gold, hallelujah has universal value. Hallelujah has no language or cultural boundaries. God has ordained it as the highest praise. It is the believers gold. It can be integrated into singing, dancing, the lifting of hands and physically bowing down for the Lord. Any way we choose to come into His presence, we should come with Hallelujahs. Whatever means or mode we choose to praise the hell out of ourselves with, we should come in with the highest praise, Hallelujah. Hallelujah is the gold that has been stolen and must be reclaimed and restored. The word Halla means to brag or boast. Jah means God. The only noun missing is you! Are you ready? Let the praise begin. Begin bragging and boasting on God. Boast on who he is and brag on what he has done. Hallelujah!

Why the Highest Praise

Gleaming from Rev. 19:1-6, which is one of the spring-board scriptures for this chapter, we discern the reason why hallelujah is the highest praise.

1. It is Redemption's and Salvation's crowned. From the foundation of the world, God had an unfolding plan of redemption to save the world. This plan is finished, and God crowned it with hallelujah. "After this I heard what sounded like the roar of a great multitude in heaven shouting: Hallelujah! Salvation and glory and power belong to God.

2. It Completes Vengeance on the Devil. This entire book is based on the premise that God provides believers with a weapon called praise to bring vengeance against Satan. Hallelujah brings to fruition that vengeance. He is defeated. "For true and just are his judgements...He had avenged on her the blood of servants. And again they shouted Hallelujah."

3. It Confirms His Kingship. Jesus came to us first as a Savior, but he will come again as a King. We praise Him now for being King of Kings and Lord of Lords. " And the four and twenty elders and the four beasts fell down and worshipped God that sat on the throne, saying, Amen; Hallelujah!

4. It Consummates Relationships With Him. When it is all said and done, if we are not in a relationship with Him, nothing else will really matter. "And a voice came out of the throne, saying, Praise our God, all ye his servants, and ye that fear him, both small and great. And I

heard as it were the voice of many waters, and as the voice of mighty thunderings, saying, Alleluia: for the Lord God Omnipotent reigneth." Hallelujah

When we think about why Hallelujah is the highest praise, we want to make sure we are in the presence of God and not in the presence of evil. There is a way to have this assurance; God gave it to us in praise. We have the privilege of praising ourselves into the presence of God, but we must first praise all the hell out of ourselves.

In closing, let me encourage you to hold onto your praise of gold. Resist the temptation to imitate and offer God a substitute. Our King Shishak, the devil, will always try to steal what does not belong to him. God alone is worthy of our most costly possession — our lives submitted to the Lordship of Jesus Christ filled with authentic praise.

Skull Practice

Chapter 11 -- Praising the Hell Out of Yourself
With the Highest Praise -- Hallelujah

1. What is the highest praise?

"Hallelujah" holds the honor of denoting the highest praise.

2. Based on Revelation 19:1-6, list four reasons why hallelujah is the highest praise.

(a) It is redemption and salvation crowned

(b) It completes vengeance on the devil

(c) It confirms His kingship

(d) It consummates relationships with Him

3. List six likenesses to gold and praise.

(a) Both gold and praise hold their value and do not depreciate

(b) Both gold and praise hold no inner impurities

(c) Both gold and praise are perfected by heat or fire

(d) Both gold and praise are valued in various individual modes and methods

(e) Both gold and praise are awesome and brilliant in appearance

(f) Both gold and praise are often imitated

4. Does "hallelujah" have language or cultural boundaries?

No. Hallelujah has universal value, and has no language or cultural boundaries.

Fill in the blanks

1. In the eyes of God, _____ is priceless. (praise)

2. Like gold, the value of our _____ and adoration to God will never depreciate. (praise)

3. Like gold, genuine _____ is pure _____. (praise) (praise)

4. Like gold, as the spirit of God "turns up the heat" during _____, the _____ we offer to God becomes more pronounced, direct and intense. (praise) (praise)

5.   Like gold, because of the beauty and liberty found in _____, it is often imitated and thus perverted. (praise)

What will be the outcome of ignoring the teaching in this chapter?

1. You will run the risk of offering God cheap imitation praise.

2. You will run the risk of undervaluing a most precious gift.

3. You miss the opportunity to experience a foretaste of glory divine.

4. You miss having the assurance of a universal communication and common denominator with Christians all over the world.

5. You will miss the opportunity to utilize what the Bible describes as a voice of triumph.

Helpful dialogue

1. Concerning praise being stolen, contemporize the biblical illustration mentioned in this chapter relative to King Shishak stealing the golden shields that Solomon made.

2. Discuss the reasons listed in this chapter based on Revelation 19:1-6 relative to why hallelujah is the highest praise.

3. Discuss a comparison between gold and praise.

4. Discuss the universality of hallelujah.

Chapter Twelve
Praising the Hell out of Yourself with a Voice of Triumph

"And they sang together by course in praising and giving thanks unto the Lord; because he is good, for his mercy endureth for ever toward Israel. And all the people shouted with a great shout, when they praised the Lord because the foundation of the house of the Lord was laid." (Ezra 3:11)

"Oh clap your hands, all ye people; shout unto God with the voice of triumph." (Psalm 47:1)

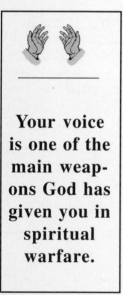

Your voice is one of the main weapons God has given you in spiritual warfare.

Your voice is one of the main weapons God has given you in spiritual warfare. You see, the devil can't stand to hear praise. Praise and the devil are incompatible. They can't operate in the same space. Because God inhabits the praises of His people, the devil must tuck his tail and leave when Almighty God shows up! Many believe the reason why praise is so displeasing to the devil is became it is a paralyzing reminder of the home, job, position and blessings he lost.

"How art thou fallen from heaven, O Lucifer, son of the morning! How art thou cut down to the ground, which didst weaken the nations! For thou hast said in thine heart, I will ascend into heaven, I will exalt my throne above the stars of God: I will

sit also upon the mount of the congregation, in the sides of the
north: I will ascend above the heights of the clouds;
I will be like the most High." (Isaiah 14:12-14)

Many theologians ascribe the above passage to Satan's ejection from heaven. In his role prior to being kicked out, the devil was a cherub, a high ranking angel in the kingdom. His responsibility included presenting praise to God. He was a beautiful angel and perfect in his ways until sin was found in him. Ezekiel describes him as follows.

Thou art the anointed cherub that covereth; and I have set
thee so: thou wast upon the holy mountain of God; thou
hast walked up and down in the midst of the stones of fire.
Thou wast perfect in thy ways from the day that
thou wast created, till iniquity was found in thee.
(Ezekiel 28:13-14)

When mankind lifts up praises to God, Satan goes crazy thinking about how far he has fallen.

He was so beautiful that his looks became a source of pride and rebellion for him. At some point, he decided that he would replace God on the high throne and receive the glory and praise due God alone. Mistake! God had to remind the devil that he was a **creature** and not the **Creator.** After sin was found in him, the devil got fired from his job; and, along with another 1/3 of the angels, was kicked out of heaven onto the earth. When mankind lifts up praises to God, Satan goes crazy thinking about how far he has fallen. This is the reason we can praise the hell out of ourselves.

Not only does lifting up a voice of triumph make Satan remember the job he once had, it also reminds him of mankind's relationship with God. Satan knows that God loves us so much that He would: fashion himself a body, come down through forty-two generations, willingly die on the cross, be buried in a borrowed tomb so that He could rise triumphantly, in order to give his crowning creation - man - the keys to death, hell and the grave! Glory to God! That alone should cause you to lift your triumphant voice in praise!

What is man, that thou art mindful of him? and the son of man, that thou visitest him? For thou hast made him a little lower than the angels, and hast crowned him with glory and honour. Thou madest him to have dominion over the works of thy hands; thou has put all things under his feet: All sheep and oxen, yea, and the beasts of the field; The fowl of the air, and the fish of the sea, and whatsoever passeth through the paths of the seas. O LORD our Lord, how excellent is thy name in all the earth! (Psalm 8:4-9)

Always remember, Satan despises your dominion, your praise, your God, and you!

Always remember, Satan despises your dominion, your praise, your God, and **you!**

There is a way to prove how much Satan hates praise. As mentioned in the introduction of this book, find someone you know that does not have any fruit on their tree. Someone who is not exhibiting any characteristics of a saved person. No matter how hard you look, you can't find a grape of kindness, an apple of love, a pear of suffering, a peach of temperance, nor an orange of goodness (Galatians 5:22-23). Their tree is bare! They try not to exhibit to them, any evidence that you possess the fruit of the spirit.

Put them in your car. Take them on a major highway and get up to a nice speed (but stay within the speed limit). Roll up all the windows and lock all the doors. Pop in an anointed praise tape, give it some volume, and watch the person begin to squinch. One person told me that he tried this acid test and the young man tried to put his head out of the car. If he could have jumped out, he would have. He couldn't stand it because the evil (demons) in him couldn't stand being in the midst of praise.

Praise, specifically warfare praise, has a similar effect on believers. I have a friend who has a warfare tape that he recommends not to listen to while driving. The power of the praise that it invokes will literally cause radical, crazy praise that will chase the *hell right out of the believer and/ or his or her presence.*

The spring board scripture printed at the beginning of this chapter comes from Ezra. He is one of the post-exilic prophets. He prophesied after the exile. This scripture deals with the setting of the second building of the Temple. This was the second temple of Israel. This was not the one that we talked about when we talked about David, and the great Temple that Solomon built.

The Israelites had been off in exile because of their sins. For seventy years they remained in the northern country of Babylon by the river Kebar, where they sat and pondered, then finally they got an opportunity to come home. They returned under the leadership of Ezra and Nehemiah, who we call the prophets of reform, and Haggai and Zechariah. There was a great revival going on with the people, and Ezra was the leader of the beginning of the revival.

And they sang together by course in praising and giving
thanks unto the Lord; because he is good, for his mercy
endureth for ever toward Israel.　And all the people shouted
with a great shout, when they praised the Lord because
the foundation of the house of the Lord was laid.　(Ezra 3:11)

This scripture was written after much labor and much work.　Even going against opposition, hard times, people talking about them, the devil being busy.　But finally the foundation of the church was laid.　Because the foundation of the church was laid, the people had something to shout about.　Now literally, this was just the foundation. We've got a roof over our heads!　Now if they could shout when they poured the basement of the church, it looks like we've got something to shout about when we've got a roof over our heads—and a chandelier over our heads.　We have something to shout about in Jesus Christ our Lord.

Several years ago, Shirley Caesar produced a gospel recording called "Shouting John."　She talks about this fellow named Shouting John who came to a sophisticated church that didn't believe in clapping their hands and saying "amen."　They certainly didn't believe in testifying and shouting.　Some of the congregation reprimanded Shouting John for doing so much shouting.　As the story goes, the deacons had to make a visit to Shouting John's home. They tried to convince Shouting John not to do so much shouting.　But no matter how much they used the art of persuasion, they could not keep Shouting John from shouting.　Shouting John told them of several stories to let them know that he indeed had something to shout about.　After relating to several deliverance experiences, Shouting John told the concerned deacons to "Hold His Mule" because he felt a shout coming on, even as they were speaking.

In essence, Shouting John told them, "Look out yonder." You see that old stump. That's where I used to drink my whiskey. But I don't drink whiskey any more because one day the Lord touched me and He lifted it from the gut of my stomach. That's why somebody had better hold my mule. He said, you see that old church house over there, and the old cabin over there. When my wife died and left me with all these children to raise, the Lord took care of me. That's why somebody needs to hold my mule.

He said when I think about all the Lord has done for me, when the doctors had laid me on the bed, but yet I'm still standing, somebody hold my mule. I imagine some of those old deacons said, "John, you ought to take that back. John, we can't have folks going around talking like that. Take it back!" I imagine John just looked at them and said, "Before I'll take it back, I'll add more to it. God has really been good to me." Take it back. John said, "Before I'll take it back I'll add more to it. God has really been good to me. Hold my mule."

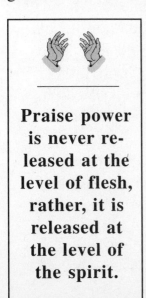

Praise power is never released at the level of flesh, rather, it is released at the level of the spirit.

The reason why some believers are offended by praise can be summarized as follows. The first reason can be labeled unregenerated logic. It appears to be foolish, and unintelligent. Leaning on our own fleshly level of understanding is silly and foolish. The wall of Jericho and any other deliverance comes from an obedient shout. God has told us that His foolish thing would confuse the wisdom of human intelligence. Praise power is never released at the level of flesh, rather, it is released at the level of the spirit. We are called to walk not in the flesh, but in the Spirit. Believers who lean on human understanding have not had their logic regenerated, therefore, will never be really free to use praise as a weapon.

The second reason is pride. Pride can be defined as loving yourself more than God. Most of us need to outwardly express praise on a daily basis, if for no other reason than to praise the hell of pride out of ourselves.

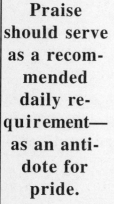

Praise should serve as a recommended daily requirement—as an antidote for pride.

Pride is one of the most deadly sins. The reason why pride is so deadly is because pride has no accountability. We can even conceal our own pride. We should not take any chances, whether we think we are proud or not; we should take a daily dose of praise as a precaution measure. Praise should serve as a recommended daily requirement—as an antidote for pride.

The third reason some are offended by praise is because of tradition and culture. There are some churches that have quietness as a part of their tradition and culture. Certainly, it is good to be quiet, because God often comes to us in a quite, still voice. However, to participate in quietness and not to participate in praise is unbiblical. God told the psalmist to tell us to make a joyful noise into the Lord (Psalm 100:1). In the 47th Psalm, we are told to clap our hands, for it represents a shout and a voice of triumph.

> *O Clap your hands, all ye people; shout unto God*
> *with the voice of triumph*
> (Psalm 47:1)

Unconfessed sin dominates the life of many believers, leaving them in a continuous backslidden posture, and not living the abundant, victorious life that has been granted to them.

The fourth reason why believers are offended by high praise is because of unconfessed sin. Unconfessed sin dominates the life of many believers, leaving them in a continuous backslidden posture, and not living the abundant, victorious life that has been granted to them. God has promised that He is "faithful and just to forgive us our sins, and to cleanse us from all unrighteousness." (I John 1:9)

David, the greatest sinner and the greatest saint of the old testament tells us, "If I regard iniquity in my heart, the Lord will not hear me." (Psalms 66:18) I believe that sometimes we need to "shout it out." There is a stain remover on the market that bears the label *Shout*. When washing clothes, you put in an extra dirty spot like around the collar of your shirts. *Shout* is used for the difficult, hard to get clean, dirty spots.

When Christ died on the cross, He pardoned us from the penalty of sin by redemption and salvation. Yet believers still have ring around the collar. The devil is still present in our lives. Satan gives us a hard time. But God has already given us the victory. We must simply raise our voices in triumph, regardless of what the situation looks like. As Christians, either we trust God or we don't. There is no middle ground.

If God said it, **He** will bring it to pass. We cannot be afraid of shouting the victory prior to the manifestation. To do so implies there is little or no faith. The opposite of faith is fear and/or unbelief. Fear is simply this: *F*alse

*E*vidence which *A*ppears *R*eal. Faith is: *F*aintlessly Accepting *I*n *T*he *H*eart God's Word. Don't faint. Don't stagger. Don't fear. The victory is already ours. We must be confident that our lifestyles are holy, so that our victory shouts will not be in vain!

One word of caution—praise plays no part in our salvation experience. This word of caution comes lest we get carried away in our praising and begin to think that we got saved because we "got our shout on." Christ already paid the price for our salvation. God wants us to give a testimony about how He brought us out of darkness, and placed us in the marvelous light. He (God) desires for us to be overcomers. In order to do that, we must open our mouths and—tell it!

> *"And they overcame him by the blood of the Lamb,*
> *and by the word of their testimony; and they loved*
> *not their lives unto death."*
> *(Revelation 12:11)*

One final example of a victorious voice of triumph says it all without any explanation from me being necessary.

> *"And* **Jesus cried with a loud voice,** *and gave*
> *up the ghost. And the veil of the temple was rent in twain*
> *from the top to the bottom. And when the centurion,*
> *which stood over against him, saw that he so*
> *cried out, and gave up the ghost, he said, Truly this man*
> *was the Son of* God." Mark 15:33-39
> (bold emphasis given by author)

Skull Practice
Chapter Twelve — Praising the Hell Out of Yourself
With a Voice of Triumph

1. List four reasons why some believers are offended by praise.
    (a)   Unregenerated logic
    (b)   Pride
    (c)   Tradition and culture
    (d)   Unconfessed sin

2. What is the role of praise in the salvation experience?
None. Praise is an experience that results from the salvation experience.

3. Why is pride one of the most deadly sins.
Pride has no accountability in the sense that you cannot get caught in the act of pride.

4. What is the solution to the deadly sin of pride?
A prescribed requirement of a daily dose of praise to serve as an antidote.

Fill in the blanks

1. Your _____ is one of the main weapons God has given the saints for spiritual warfare. (voice)

2. Lifting up a _____ of triumph makes Satan remember the job he held in God's Kingdom. (voice)

3.   Lifting up a _____ of triumph reminds Satan of mankind's relationship with God. (voice)

4.   God said in Psalm 47:1, "O clap your hands, all ye people; shout unto God with the _____ of triumph." (voice)

What will be the outcome of ignoring the teaching in this chapter?

1.   Your testimony will be limited.

2.   You will be in disobedience to God's word.

3.   You will forfeit victory after victory.

4.   You will be less than an overcomer.

Helpful dialogue

1.   Experiment with the acid test suggested in this chapter to prove that evil and praise are incompatible.

2.   Discuss a rewritten version of "Shouting John" based on your personal testimony.

3.   Discuss the author's assertion that God is so faithful, that believers can shout the victory prior to the manifestation.

4.   Discuss the ramification of verbal testimonies versus silent living testimonies.

Conclusion

Praising the Hell Out of Yourself

Praising the Hell Out of Yourself is about coming into His presence with the power through praise to cast out evil. Prayerfully, in reading this book, you have concluded that there is indeed tremendous power in both prayer and praise. It is not enough to simply realize the power. God has given us the knowledge to invoke the power — the power to praise the hell out of ourselves.

As God remarkably created us in His image for His pleasure, He gave us free reign to choose between good and evil. In many instances, we have chosen evil. But God in His overflowing abundance of grace and mercy, gives His children another chance. He gives us another chance to get it right.

Praising the Hell Out of Yourself describes twelve ways that God has graciously given all His children to get it right. God could have very easily removed the evil himself (Zephaniah 3:15). Or God could have very easily removed the evil-doers (Hosea 9:17). But because of his unfailing love for us, God chose to allow us to personally take part in the self-cleansing process — Praising the Hell Out of Ourselves.

"Praising the Hell out of Yourself through the Dance" describes how the dance, when appropriately offered to God in praise, has a powerful, liberating effect. The Dance is only one of many forms of praise. The key is the motive which should always be "to give God the glory."

"Praising the Hell out of Yourself with Lifted Hands" explains how God gave us holy hands so that in praising Him with them all the world can see. We should worship with our hands before we start working with our hands. We should lift up our hands in surrender to Him and love for Him. Through God, our holy hands can be used as weapons against evil.

"Praising the Hell out of Yourself with Thanksgiving" should be second nature to the believer because all we have to do is to step back and think of how God has delivered us so many times out of so many situations. If we can think, we can thank.

"Praising the Hell out of Yourself with Righteousness and a Holy Offering" explains how we must seek righteousness through confession before we can enter into God's presence with praise.

"Praising the Hell out of Yourself with Singing and Music" reveals how God created music for the express purpose of honoring and worshipping Him. The scripture admonishes all of us to make a joyful noise unto the Lord. This is our responsibility, regardless of our so-called musical talent.

"Praising the Hell out of Yourself with the Tithe" teaches that God will interact with and on our behalf when we worship Him through the giving of the tithe to His church. Tithing will put you in the right relationship with God so that you can praise hellish spirits out of your life.

"Praising the Hell out of Yourself in Time of Trouble" emphasizes that we should praise God in the midst of our circumstances. Intense praise during times of adversity can change the wrath of evil men or wicked situations.

"Praising the Hell out of Yourself with Childlike Character" portrays how we should strive to possess the genuine purity and honesty of children so that we can enter into the presence of the Lord.

"Praising the Hell out of Yourself with a Sacrifice" emphasizes that sacrifice is a prerequisite to worship. We must be willing to give up our best to truly receive THE best.

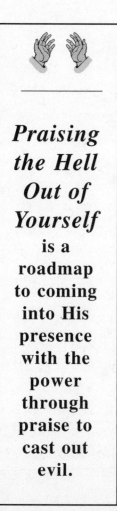

Praising the Hell Out of Yourself **is a roadmap to coming into His presence with the power through praise to cast out evil.**

"Praising the Hell out of Yourself through the use of Names" emphatically states that we will never fully understand all there is about our Father. However, through the use of His names, we can better define Him. God has promised us that we can invoke His power by calling on His name.

"Praising the Hell out of Yourself with the Highest Praise - Hallelujah" reveals that praise is a weapon given to saints to use in spiritual warfare against Satan. God receives all praise genuinely offered to Him, regardless of its intensity. However, we must be careful not to offer Him imitation praise. Hallelujah has been ordained as the highest praise.

"Praising the Hell out of Yourself with a Voice of Triumph" triumphantly exclaims that your voice is one of the main weapons God has given you in spiritual warfare. When believers lift up praises to God, Satan goes crazy thinking about how far he has fallen. We must never get carried away thinking that we play a role in our salvation experience. Although free to us, Christ paid the price for our salvation.

Praising the Hell Out of Yourself is a roadmap to coming into His presence with the power through praise to cast out evil.

APPENDIX

A Dramatization

"Praising the Hell Out of Yourself"

PRAISING THE HELL OUT OF YOURSELF

CAST OF CHARACTERS

Pastor	Young minister recently called to his first church
Mother Wimbush	Well respected Mother in the church
Dr. Nathaniel Wimbush	Son of Mother Wimbush. Well-known Neurosurgeon and currently a non-believer
Sis. Betty	Church member - New convert. Eager to learn —regular attender of Sunday School class.
Bro. Paul	Widower, Father. Mentorer in the church
Teacher (Sis. Sybil Strong)	Sunday School teacher and counselor
Dr. Mozell	Clinic Doctor and Christian
Brenda	Church member going through trials raising a teenage son

PRAISING THE HELL OUT OF YOURSELF

ACT I

Narrator: It is Friday evening, Prayer Meeting time at the Praise Him Baptist Church in Atlanta. A young minister has recently been called to serve as Pastor at this well established neighborhood church. He humbly goes to God in praise and prayer.

Opening Scene - (Young pastor enters church, while looking and walking around he silently admires the beautiful sanctuary. He pauses, he began speaking as though he is thinking out loud - . Smiling.)

Pastor: Praise the Lord! Praise the Lord! Let everything that have breath praise ye the Lord. Father, you've been so good to me and I thank you for it. You've blessed me to pastor this church and I don't take it lightly — I can't. You said, "Where much is given, much is expected. You deserve the best. I owe everything to you. And you, my Lord, deserve the highest praise — Hallelujah!

Lord, I have a burden for your people. In the six months since I've been called to serve here, I've seen some of your people growing, I've seen other struggling, and yet others are suffering. Please help me to be a good servant.. I know you're able. Help me to always put you first.

When the congregation look my way, help them to see not me, but you. And oh, if by chance, my hair turns prematurely white. Let it not be white from worry, but a symbol of wisdom and the crown of glory to come when we meet face to face.

Jehovah Shammah, the Lord who is present with me, I praise you. Yadah! I lift my hands to honor you. I surrender all.

(Church members begin arriving at the sanctuary for Prayer Service. The first on the scene is Mother Wimbush and her Son, Dr. Wimbush. She and her son come in with Flowers and fresh water for the pastor)

Mother: Good evening pastor, You doing okay this evening?.

Pastor: Yes ma'am, I couldn't be better. You came to prepare the place for the evening Bible Study, didn't you? We really appreciate your thoughtfulness, Mother Wimbush

Mother: Just want to freshen up the place a bit.
These flowers ought to last through this
weekend. (places flowers in container)

You know pastor, I want you to know how
Happy we are that the Lord sent you our
way. We have been waiting so long for a
Pastor. (*laughingly*)   Of course now, we
didn't know you'd be so young.   I got
shoes older than you. But that does not
matter one bit. We thank God for you, just
the same.   *Pastor nods and walks out of
the room)*

Son can you give me a hand here for a
minute. (*They start to arrange the altar
area and she began reminiscing)*

I remember when your father and I use to do
this every Saturday together. You remind
me so much of your father. I'm proud of
the fine man you've become.   Thank you
Lord!

(*Mother motions for her son to come help her)*

Mother: (To son) Son, it's so good to have you back
in church where you belong.

Dr. Wimbush: Alright mom. Don't get no ideas.
I'm only here to get a break from your
nagging me so much about church.

Church, church, church   ... you practically
live at the church. But that's not for me.

Mother: I remember when you were a little boy.

Dr. Wimbush: Oh there you go again.

Mother: Yes, I was so proud of you,. Your Sunday
School teachers just loved having you in
their classes. You always knew the answers
and raised such thought-provoking
questions.

Dr. Wimbush: I was just a child then. I didn't know
any better.   Now I have learned <u>not</u> to
volunteer information.

Mother: Yes, you loved to study about Jesus and
couldn't wait for Vacation Bible School.
Why, that very attitude is what God wants
from all His children. God wants us to
come to Him with a childlike character.

*(Mother and son are unaware that the
Pastor re-enters the room and overhears the
conversation - he looks concerned)*

Dr. Wimbush: I've grown from that stuff Mother.
I am an accomplished physician now.   I've
been exposed to some of the best minds in
the world. I'm my own person. I've pulled
myself up by my own bootstraps. I'm really

living large now.   Now, I **Think**
Differently.

Mother: Now Nathaniel, Sister Mozell's son is a
doctor too. And he still thinks that Jesus is
special. He comes to church EVERY
Sunday.

Dr. Wimbush: It is obvious how Dr. Mozell thinks.
He works the Emergency Room at
Grady…a county clinic. I, on the other
hand, am the Head Neurological Surgeon at
EMORY Hospital. (There is a difference.)

Mother: Well, I know, as my pastor say all the time.
If you can THINK, you can THANK (God
that is).   And you ain't above that.   I didn't
raise you that way.   And don't you get
sassy with me … with your long tall self.
I am still your mama.

Son, **I** think it's time you get back to the
real FACTS OF LIFE. (Opens Bible)
"In the beginning was the Word, and the
Word was with God, and the Word was God
…"

(Other members of the church start to arrive)

Pastor: Come in church. Come in. Let's come into
His presence with singing and praise.

Devotion Leader: Let's stand church and sing our
                          favorite praise song: "Lift Jesus Higher"

Song: Higher, Higher!   Higher, Higher, Higher, Higher
         Higher, Higher! Lift Jesus Higher!
         Lower, Lower!   Lower, Lower, Lower, Lower
         Lower, Lower! Stomp Satan Lower!
         Super, Super!   Super, Super, Super, Super
         Super, Super! God has supernatural power!

Scripture:

            "And they sang together by course in
            praising and giving thanks unto the LORD;
            because he is good, for his mercy endureth
            for ever toward Israel. And all the people
            shouted with a great shout, when they
            praised the LORD, because the foundation
            of the house of the LORD was laid.."
            (Ezra 3:11)

Prayer:

            Lord, I thank you for your many blessings.
            I thank you for my church, my Pastor and
            my family.   Thank you for your forgiveness
            of our sins. Help us to love one another as
            you love us. We ask it all in your Son's
            name.   Amen.

Teacher: Pastor, I stand at this time with a testimony.
                  The Bible says in Phillipians 4:6 "Be
                  careful for nothing: but in every thing by

prayer and supplication with thanksgiving let your requests be made known unto God." God is listening. He will take care of his children. It doesn't matter how big or small the problem may be, God is the answer.

Yes, I spend a lot of time teaching and counseling the members of this church. When we didn't have a Pastor, I almost thought for a minute I had received the calling. The Lord soon revealed to me that I was just "Standing in the Place" 'till HE worked it out.

I know Lord, you're going to work it out. Just like you worked out the situations in the lives of our members. You took care of Mother Wimbush when her son Nathaniel went off to college and she was left alone. And remember how Bro. Paul was so worried about his daughter when she was young and ran away from home. He was in so much pain when his wife died. But you sent his church members to be a source of support for him. My mama always say that I had the gift of GAB.

ALL: Yes   (All the church members readily agrees)

Teacher: I guess I do talk quite a bit sometime. Bro.

Paul, come on up here and tell the folks about your own daughter. (shyly) I guess that's all I have to say.   I think I'll take my seat.

Bro. Paul: Lord, I want to say thank you. Thank you for my family!   I am so proud of my daughter.   She's married and living in New York with her three wonderful children.. And Lord I thank you for how you're working in their lives everyday.   Such a wonderful family.   Thank you!

Mother : I'm proud to have my son, Dr. Nathaniel Wimbush, Head NEGRO Surgeon at Emory Hospital

Son: Head Neuro Surgeon, MOTHER.   That's Neuro Surgeon.

Mother: Anyway, my son has come back to the church where he belongs. I always prayed he would come back to the church. It does not matter why, I am just happy he is here and I hope it is to stay.

Pastor: Let's all stand and close in a word of prayer.

(After prayer, members begin to leave. As Teacher goes to the door, Sis. Betty rushes after her)

Sis. Betty: Sis. Strong, Sis. Strong, are you ok? You weren't your usual self on Sunday morning. And today you walked into the room and didn't say a word to anyone. Are you ok?

Teacher: (With a very sad face). I'm fine.

Sis. Betty: But you don't look fine.

Teacher: Don't worry about me. I'll be ok. ... Later ... If I'm lucky (Begins crying)

Sis. Betty: I knew something was wrong. What can I do?

Teacher: Nothing! I said Nothing! I'm fine!

Sis. Betty: I know I'm no rocket scientist, but I know something is very wrong. You have always been the one there for me and everyone in our class. Whenever we had a problem, you were there with a scripture of comfort. Sometimes we just needed to talk, but we always knew you would be there for us, with the right words at the right time. So please, let **me** help **you** this time.

Teacher: You can't help me. Nobody can help me.

Sis. Betty: That's not what you're always telling us. You would say "there's nothing too large or too small for God to handle." So what's the problem?

Teacher: The problem is ME. I went to my doctor
last week and he told me that I have a Brain
Tumor.   (Begins to cry) Me, with a Brain
Tumor.

Sis. Betty: I am so sorry to hear this news. (Hugs
teacher)   Let it out. It's ok to cry.

Teacher: What am I going to do? This is just awful.
(Takes keys out of her purse and lays them
on the table as she looks for a tissue to wipe
her eyes.) Oh I'm so embarrassed, I must
seem out of control.   Excuse me while I go
to the ladies room. I want to wash my face.
I need a moment.

(Teacher leaves the room)

Sis. Betty: (*Pacing and frantically searching*) Lord,
help me!   What should I do?   What should
I say?   She always know what to do.   I've
got to do something. I've got to say
something. But what? I know, my teacher
always has her Bible with her? (Locates
Bible) Here it is. Now what's next. Let's
see. What do I turn to? She always told us
that we need to memorize scriptures.   She
could just ramble off one verse after
another.   I guess she memorized the whole
Bible. (Turns pages of the Bible)   Ok,

nothing looks familiar at the beginning.
Nor the middle. Or even at the end.   She
could always go straight to whatever
Scripture she needed.   Ok this is NOT
going to work (places Bible down),

So what would Teacher do?   I know.   She
would PRAY.   But I don't know a lot of
big words.   I don't know what to say to
God.   I guess I'll just do what I always do
— just talk.

Okay God, my Sunday School teacher
needs help.   Please help her.   I don't know
what to do or what to say.   But she always
tells us that YOU are the answer.-She
encourages us and tell us that all we need to
do is to go to you in prayer.   Lord, you may
not know me all that well.   But you do
know Sis. Strong, my Sunday School
teacher.   She is a good person — real
smart, and she is a dedicated Christian..

Lord help her, please.   Her doctor told her
she has a brain tumor.   She is hurting so
much now that she can't think to talk to you
like usual.   So that's where I come in.   She
is single, and live so far away from her
immediate family , but help her understand
we are her family, church family and we all
care for her sincerely.   Please make her feel
better.   Amen.

>   (Looking around and at watch) I wonder
>   what's taking her so long. I'd better go
>   check on her. She seemed pretty upset.

(Sis. Betty leaves)

(Teacher and Dr. Wimbush enter from opposite
directions)

Teacher: Oh excuse me, Nathaniel, I mean Dr.
Wimbush.

Dr. Wimbush: Oh girl, I am still Nathaniel to you.
How are you Sylvia?

Teacher: I'm good

Dr. Wimbush: Still ....Single

Teacher: Still........ Single.

Dr. Wimbush: What's the matter, you seem upset?

Teacher: Very

Dr. Wimbush: Can I help?

Teacher: I wish. I'm not sure anyone can help me at
this point

Dr. Wimbush: I'll try

Teacher: Okay, you're a doctor (Sighs) You're use
to just the hard facts. I've been diagnosed
with a Brain Tumor

Dr. Wimbush: I'm sorry.   The Prognosis?

Teacher: Not Good.   It is inoperable.

Dr. Wimbush: That is Serious

Teacher: Very!

Dr. Wimbush: I'm so sorry!

Teacher -   Me Too. What a fine time for this to
happen. Just when I thought I was
beginning to enjoy life.   I met this really
nice Christian man and things look so
promising for us. For the very first time,
I'm in love and I feel love - and now it's all
complicated. I can't dump this problem on
him.. This is just awful.

Dr. Wimbush: That is a bit much. But maybe he'll
understand. You said he was a Christian,
that should count for something.

Teacher: That is ALL that really does count
Nathaniel.. (as she re-composes)

(Dr. Mozell enters)

Dr. Mozell: Oh, there you are, Wimbush

Teacher: (hurriedly) I've got to go now (leaves)

Dr. Mozell: Wimbush, I was hoping we got a chance to talk before I left town. I am attending that conference in DC this weekend and wanted to run over a few concerns relating the incident at the hospital this week.

Dr. Wimbush: You mean, the Nesby case?

Dr. Mozzel: Yes, what went wrong?

Dr. Wimbush: Look, I followed all the procedures, I consulted the finest specialist in the nation. I studied and re-evaluated the situation and I certainly made the best decision. Look, life is a science, if the heart beat stops, the blood stop flowing and that is the end of the road. You're dead. It's a science I tell you. A science. I am the Best surgeon in this region and I know I did the best thing. I don't take loosing a patient lightly, I'm good at my job and I am an excellent, well qualified and certified doctor. I don't understand it. My colleagues all agree with me, I did the RIGHT thing. I did everything right. I don't know what went wrong.

Dr. Mozzel: Hey man, don't be so hard on yourself. You're human. It happens.

Dr. Wimbush: (Angrily) Look, I am Good at what I do. And like I said, Life is a Science and Science is an absolute. When things don't go right - something went wrong. That is what happened in the operating room. Something went wrong and it is not my fault.

Dr Mozzell: Nathaniel, sometimes, even when we do all we can and know to do it does not always work out . Ultimately, it is not in our hands, It is in God's hand.

Dr. Wimbush: Oh NO! You too! You are an educated, intelligent man Mozzell. I know you spend a good bit of time here at the church but don't loose sight of what you are. You're a trained scientist. You studied to become a doctor.

Look, I know the people here believe, take my mom, she is here so much she should be able to take people straight to heaven herself. But what we do is real ... NOT Magic!

Dr. Mozzell: I don't know about you brother, but what I do is nothing compared to what God can and will do. What has happened to you?

(Both doctors leave, continuing to talk to each other)

Teacher: (to self) I must have left my keys in here.
                 Let me just look.

(Teacher enters sanctuary, locates keys and puts them in
her purse. As she wipes her eyes, Pastor enters)

Pastor: Oh sister Sylvia, what's wrong?

Teacher: (trying to hold back the tears) I'm fine!
                 I've got to go now. (Teacher hurriedly
                 leaves.)

Pastor stands, looking bewildered)

Bro. Paul: Oh Pastor, I hate to trouble you, but do you
                 have a moment?

Pastor: Always. No trouble at all.

Bro. Paul: Well, back in the service this evening. I
                 guess I was too full of pride to admit that
                 things were not so good for my daughter
                 right now. I wish Sis. Betty hadn't brought
                 her name up. It's just that it caught me off
                 guard. You see the truth is that my daughter
                 and her three children have come back
                 home. She and her husband are getting a
                 divorce. Why me, God?   Why me?

                 Why do all the bad things seem to come my
                 way? I go to church. I pay my tithe. I am
                 a good person. Just at the point in my life

where I should be having some time to myself, my daughter comes home with not one, but three babies. I'm too old for this. The noise, the crying.... I can't take it.

My wife died a year ago. We had been married twenty-four years and did everything together. Why did she have to leave me? For the past year, I buried myself deep into my job. But this week was different. I walked into the office on Monday morning and was given my pink slip. Now I don't have a job. What am I supposed to do — start over at my age? The bills don't stop coming because I don't have a job. What am I going to do? I'm not about to ask for charity. I wasn't raised on handouts and I'm not about to start now.

Lord, what do I do now? (Places hands on face).

Pastor: You hold steadfast and pray, Bro. Paul. That's what you do. Pride is one of the seven deadly sins. It can grab hold of you and won't let go. You just PRAY that hell right out of yourself!

(Pastor and Bro. Paul leaves stage)

ACT II

Narrator: It is Sunday Morning, almost time for Worship Service at the Praise Him Baptist Church. Mother Wimbush hurries in to talk with Pastor.

Mother: Pastor, Bro. Paul didn't make it to teach his Sunday School class this morning. That's not like him.   I guess he had some sort of emergency.

Pastor: Umm.   I'll give him a call later. (Pastor turns)

(Mother goes to water the flowers from Friday and place water for the Pastor to drink)

(Members enter sanctuary, greeting each other)

(Pastor calls service to order)

Pastor: O how blessed we are to be His children. He loves us one and all. We owe Him praise.

If you think, you can thank. If you can thank, you can praise. If you can praise, you can worship. If you can't praise, then there is something wrong with your thinking. The songwriter put it this way: "When I look back over my life and I think things over, I can truly say that I've been blessed. I've got a testimony.

We need to praise God for all things.

I often hear from many of the people I talk with. After they shared their problem with me, they come to the conclusion that: I know I'll get thru this. I need to approach this thing differently. I'll be fine. I will work it all out. Well I am here to tell you that "There is NOTHING we can do or have in our OWN power."

We have no power. When we get to thinking that we don't need God's power twins — Grace and Mercy — to save, deliver and protect us, that's proof in itself that we've got hell in us. Satan has done his job — to make us think that WE have the power.

Satan lives in hell. And so SATAN IS HELL. And wherever SATAN is, hell is also. And when let our guards down and allow Satan to come into our lives, what we need to do is PRAISE THE HELL OUT OF OURSELVES.

Can I get a witness?

Our sermon text is taken from Psalm 47:1: "O clap your hands all ye people. Shout unto God with the voice of triumph."

Sermon Title: Praising the Hell Out of
Yourself

Church, we are blessed!   God is good (all
the time).   And all the time (God is good).
We can just look around and see the
manifestation of His goodness all around us.
No, we don't have to look far.   He makes
his presence known to His people.

Another thing we must remember is that He
keeps his promise.   He said He would never
leave or forsake us.   He said He would send
his Holy Spirit to comfort and guide us.
And this He did.   Not only did He leave His
Holy Spirit (the Comforter), but He left
instructions for us to call on Him. God's
name is powerful in praise and prayer.
Therefore, all our prayers and praise ought
to be done in His name. When we come
before His presence, we ought to be coming
in His name.

Church, this is a time of joy.   A time of
celebration.   A time of victory – triumphant
victory.   Satan is defeated.   Our God lives!
The scripture says "Clap your hands all ye
people." We are all His people.   He created
us. He sustains us.   He is our all and all.
Let us give Him praise.

Let us forever use the power He has given
us through His Holy Spirit. That is the

power to stump Satan dead in his tracks through praising the living God. You see, the devil can't stand to hear praise. Praise and the devil are incompatible. They can't operate in the same space. Because God inhabits the praises of His people, the devil must tuck his tail and leave when Almighty God shows up!

When we come to worship, we are coming to God's party. We should bring something of meaning to the party as a gift for the honoree. The only gift that He asks for and that we are capable of giving is PRAISE.

However, let us not forget that praise plays no part in our salvation experience. We don't want to get carried away in our praising and begin to think that we got saved because we "got our shout on." Christ already paid the price for our salvation. God wants us to give a testimony about how He brought us out of darkness, and placed us in the marvelous light. He (God) desires for us to be overcomers. In order to do that, we must open our mouths and–TELL IT! SHOUT IT! SING IT!

"When the spirit of the Lord comes upon my heart, I will SING"

(Nathaniel Wimbush jumps to his feet)

Dr. Wimbush: Lord please forgive me!   I know
you are all powerful.   I didn't mean to steal
your praise by taking credit for what you
have done in my life.   I owe my life to you.
Thank you!   I love you Lord.

You blessed me with the ability and
knowledge and I perceived it as power.
And more and more I began to rely on my
power. Lord, as you made it clear to me
again this morning, I have no power. Who
am I to question your judgment? Lord I
have no power over life and death.   Lord,
without you as head of my life, I am
nothing. But oh lord, with you by my side,
there is no limit to my ability.   AS LONG
AS I PUT YOU FIRST.

Pastor: "When the spirit of the Lord comes upon
my heart, I will SHOUT"

(Mother jumps up praising God for saving her son.)

Pastor: Praise the Lord church.   Bro. Nathaniel has
been snatched from the hands of Satan.
Let's give the Lord praise.

Teacher: Pastor, I have a confession to make to God
and to this church.   I always considered
myself to be a good Christian, a good
worker in the church.   Practically, every
time the church door was open, I was here.

Member: We know that's right.

Teacher: I've done all I could to keep God's
                 commandments. I study my Bible daily.
                 And I don't hesitate to share a Scripture
                 with anyone I meet.

Member: You can say that again.

Teacher: I did everything I could to help everyone.   I
                 knew my Spiritual Gift was Encouragement
                 and Helps.   And I know I have a strong
                 passion for people.

Member: Then what's to confess?

Teacher: My confession is that I've allowed the devil
                 to take a stronghold in my life.

(A loud gasp is heard from the congregation, and then
silence)

                 I did not realize that I was practicing
                 Christianity in everyone else's life BUT my
                 own. It is very easy to tell others what they
                 should be doing. It's another thing to be
                 able to put it into practice yourself

                 I found out this week that I have a brain
                 tumor.   All week, I've been worrying and
                 worrying about my own condition. If it had
                 been someone else, I would have probably
                 said something like "Cast your cares upon

Him," "Have Faith," or "God won't put on us no more than we can bear."

I allowed Satan to remove God's words from my heart, and replace them with fear and doubt. Lord, I am so sorry. In time of trouble is when I should be praising you even more.

(To Satan) Get away from me Satan. There's no place here for you. All praises to God on high.

Pastor: Praise the Lord, Saints. Another warrior has praised Satan out of her life. It's a fact: Satan can't stand to hear praise.

"When the spirit of the Lord comes upon my heart, I will PRAY"

Bro. Paul: Pastor, I just can't sit hear any longer and I know I shared my concerns in private with you earlier. But I just want to thank the Lord for opening my eyes today. When my wife died a year ago, I didn't do nothing but complain about being alone. And now that my daughter and grandchildren have come home, I've been complaining about folks being in the house. I've been complaining about losing my job. I've been so busy complaining that I didn't even see when Satan sneaked into my life.

I was late getting to church this morning because my grandchild fell and hurt herself. We rushed her to the hospital and there I prayed and prayed that she would be alright,. It was then that I realized that what I thought was a bad situation was a blessing in disguise. I didn't realize how precious each moment with my family was. Lord, thank you for opening my eyes.

Lord, you sent my daughter and grandchildren back to me. Although I love them, I even complained about that. Lord you were answering my prayer of loneliness and I didn't even hear you. When I lost my job, I thought I was no longer useful and you even answered that situation. Both my daughter and my grandchildren need me. They need me to nurture and guide them in your Perfect Will. Lord God I thank you. I praise your Holy and Righteous name.

Brenda: (from audience) I didn't even know I had so much hell in me until now. Praise God, I can release it today.

I can see now that I allowed Satan's ugly spirit to reside in my soul. I have to release it today. Lord, I thank you too for this church, especially for this moment. It took all I had for me to come to church this morning. I woke up filled with so much anger. You see, around one a.m., I got this phone call from the city jail. (Congregation gasps).

My Matt was arrested last night for possession of marijuana.   I was beside myself.   In spite of all the positive things I tied to do with my son, it had to turn out this way. There I was, trying to bail my son out of the cesspool of life. I was embarrassed and humiliated. I felt I had failed as a parent.

All I could think of was that it was a good thing I couldn't get my hands on him at that moment because .... (sniffle) Oh Lord, I could not find it in my heart to be understanding, not to mention, forgiving.   I didn't deserve this.   Why was this happening to me? Was I being punished? Was God angry with me?

It took a lot of soul searching but now I can say, "Praise God for the things that did not happen."   Matt could have been killed. Someone else could have been killed. Maybe this arrest kept him from even bigger trouble.   I don't know exactly what the lesson in this situation is right now, but I serve a God who is worthy of all the praise, even if I don't always understand the situation. I trust God and I know He won't put any more on me than I can bear. And that's why I can praise the hell out of myself through the dance. (She dances)

Pastor: "When the Spirit of the Lord comes within my heart, I will DANCE."

Church, we have a lot of reasons to thank God. Let's give him some more praise. We must NOT be ashamed, but stand tall and claim the triumphant victory as we PRAISE THE HELL OUT OF OURSELVES."

Heh, heh, heh! I feel so good right now, I just can't hold it bak. I have to do it. For the Lord, I have to do it. You know, when you're fool-struck for the Lord, you can do things that don't make sense to everybody. But it is not everybody that I am trying to please. I have to run a victory lap for the Lord because there is triumphant victory here on this day. TO GOD BE ALL PRAISE! LET US PRAISE THE HELL OUT OF OURSELVES!

(Contagious Praise to God is seen all over the congregation through the dance, holy hands, laps, shouts, cries, prayer, etc.)

OTHER *EXCITING* TITLES
by George O. McCalep, Jr.

ORMAN PRESS Presents Church Growth and Spiritual Development
Resources by George O. McCalep, Jr.

Spiritual Training that Makes a Difference!

Faithful Over a Few Things   19.95
Seven Critical Church Growth Principles
ISBN 0-9652262-0-4

Breaking the Huddle   14.95
12 Messages on How to be Faithful Over the
  Seven Critical Principles of Church Growth
ISBN 0-9652262-1-2

Growing Up to the Head   19.95
10 Growth Essentials to Becoming a Better
  Christian and Church Member
ISBN 0-8952262-3-9

Stir Up the Gifts   24.95
Empowering Believers for Victorious
  Living and Ministry Tasks
ISBN 0-9652262-7-1

Sin in the House   19.95
Ten Crucial Church Problems with
  Cleansing Solutions
1-89-1773-06-2

Available at all LifeWay Bookstores, other select local Christian bookstores, and
at www.ormanpress.com.

Orman Press, Inc.
770-808-0999 or 1-800-561-0439